D0984441

DISCARDED

Gertrude Stein Is
Gertrude Stein Is Gertrude Stein

HER LIFE AND WORK

 Gertrude Stein Is Gertrude

Stein Is Gertrude Stein

HER LIFE AND WORK

BY W.G. ROGERS

Illustrated with Photographs

THOMAS Y. CROWELL COMPANY   NEW YORK

Copyright © 1973 by W. G. ROGERS

All rights reserved. Except for use in a review, the reproduction or utilization of this work in any form or by any electronic, mechanical, or other means, now known or hereafter invented, including xerography, photocopying, and recording, and in any information storage and retrieval system is forbidden without the written permission of the publisher. Published simultaneously in Canada by Fitzhenry & Whiteside Limited, Toronto.

DESIGNED BY JILL SCHWARTZ

Manufactured in the United States of America

Library of Congress Cataloging in Publication Data
Rogers, William Garland, 1896–
     Gertrude Stein is Gertrude Stein is Gertrude Stein.
     (Women of America)
     SUMMARY: A biography of the American author and art collector who was a prominent figure on the literary scene in early twentieth-century Paris.
     Bibliography: p.
     1. Stein, Gertrude, 1874–1946—Juv. lit. [1. Stein, Gertrude, 1874–1946.
2. Authors, American]
I. Title.
PS3537.T323Z795   818'.5'209 [B]   72-7555
ISBN 0-690-32585-1

1 2 3 4 5 6 7 8 9 10

WOMEN OF AMERICA

Milton Meltzer, Editor

This is dedicated to the city that Gertrude Stein
called "my home town," the city where
Gertrude Stein did her being and existing and
going on and thinking and writing and
living and at the sad last dying . . .
To the city of Paris.

Foreword

Over many years I have talked about Gertrude Stein with many people, some still alive and some now dead. For information, opinions and insights of all sorts I am indebted to Sylvia Beach, Mrs. Florence Bradley, Natalie Clifford Barney, Marie Laurencin, Joseph Barry, and Maurice Darantière, all in Paris, and to Baroness Pierlot and her son Count François d'Aiguy in Bilignin and Culoz; in this country, to Robert Coates, Virgil Thomson, Carl Van Vechten, Thornton Wilder and others. I have been privileged to consult the abundant Stein files in the Beinecke Rare Book and Manuscript Library at Yale. The curator, Dr. Donald Gallup, represents the Stein literary estate.

I have also read the several excellent biographies. But I

have mostly depended on Gertrude Stein's own writing; on her many letters to my wife, Mildred Weston, and me . . . all now at Yale; on our many letters from Alice B. Toklas, also at Yale; and on my talks and again my wife's with Gertrude Stein and Miss Toklas in Paris, Nîmes, Bilignin, New York, Springfield, Massachusetts, and elsewhere. All the quotations in the following pages, except for the few otherwise noted, are from Gertrude Stein herself. So are the chapter headings.

I met Gertrude Stein in 1917. I was such a youngster she called me Kiddy or Kiddie . . . her spelling was unorthodox. When I married she called my wife and me the Kiddies. A warm and dear friendship developed. I have tried, and I think successfully, not to let this relationship with Gertrude Stein the person affect my judgment of Gertrude Stein the writer.

W. G. ROGERS
Greenwood Farm
Gallitzin, Pennsylvania
January 1973

Contents

Illustrations

Gertrude Stein Is Gertrude Stein Is Gertrude Stein

HER LIFE AND WORK

1 *I have lived half my life in Paris, not the half that made me but the half in which I made what I made.*

—WHAT ARE MASTERPIECES

As a contradictory and paradoxical figure, it would be hard to find anyone in American letters to match Gertrude Stein.

She was laughed at madly and wildly praised. She was cheered for revitalizing English and reviled for abusing it. Her writing was supposedly incomprehensible yet it was generally comprehended. She wrote for the few and won over the many. She labored in France and reaped the rewards in the United States. She was a dreamer and a visionary yet she acquired a fortune. She was unknown one day and a celebrity the day after. She came last to the starting line and was first over the finish line. If writing were racing, no dopester would have bet a penny on Gertrude Stein at any time during her first fifty years. So he would have missed out on one of the biggest literary jackpots of the century.

Every writer longs secretly or openly for his day in the limelight. Gertrude Stein longed for hers candidly. She had it, too, and it lasted for months. It began in the fall of 1934 and ended the following spring. It was the wonderful, incredible flowering of a fantastic career. In a sense she was nothing before that time, in a sense she was everything afterward. She could be compared to some autos advertised today: accelerate from a dead stop to sixty miles an hour in one minute.

Gertrude Stein was born in the United States but after seven or eight years of college and graduate study she settled in Paris. "Paris is my home town," she wrote. There she carried on the incessant, killing struggle to write and be recognized as a writer. The grand reward came in America —"my country," as she said. The Gertrude Stein writing that people did not understand, she once remarked, was precisely the writing that piqued a reader's curiosity and drove him to pick up her books. We may say the same thing about Gertrude Stein in person. What people didn't know about her piqued public curiosity and helped draw the crowds to see and hear for themselves.

Everybody read things about her but hardly anybody read things by her. People in America heard secondhand rumors and reports and tantalizing hearsay. They were sometimes favorable, sometimes neutral and sometimes hostile. She collected the craziest kind of painting, she wrote what no one could understand, she butchered the English language, she was conceited, she was brilliant, she was a fake, she was a publicity hound, she was the greatest literary innovator of her generation.

2

Some of this might be true, all of it couldn't be. She assembled a priceless collection of Pablo Picasso paintings. But what fixes her name immovably in her time is her writing. She was a dedicated experimenter. She used English as it had never been used before. She got right down to the root problem of prose composition: the separate, individual, isolated word. She took the word, she hefted it, she smelled it, she identified its color, she examined the shape of it, she caressed and fondled it, and she gave it a job to do. Countless writers learned from her how to simplify and clarify and eliminate dross. She was a theorist, a planner, as well as a doer. She examined the nature of sentences and paragraphs and punctuation. She wrote a book on *How to Write* and she considered *What Are Masterpieces*. And of course she was bitterly attacked and mercilessly ridiculed. Words should make sense in the age-old way, her angry detractors cried. She was just a mindless mill grinding out meaningless tomes. She never knew when to stop, never knew that enough is enough. Her most obvious offense, in the opinion of the critics she infuriated, was her repeated repetitions. If she made a point once, she had to make it again and again, they charged. The famous example is her "Rose is a rose is a rose is a rose."

On October 24, 1934, she returned to America for the fiᵣt time in thirty years. She didn't get a ticker-tape parade up Broadway. That alone was lacking in the fabulous, breathtaking hero's welcome accorded to this riddle and puzzle fresh from Paris. She was here for a cross-country lecture tour. A swarm of reporters met her aboard ship and bombarded her with questions. It was a boxing match. They didn't spare her . . . a left to the jaw, a right, a haymaker, and not a few below the belt. She won every round. Her short, stout, sturdy figure, her broad smile, her genial laughter, her ready replies, her quick wit, her genius at parrying the most prying and challenging queries fascinated the newsmen. They forgot all about the tall tales they had heard. Gertrude Stein was splendidly Gertrude Stein and they loved it. Their stories and her photo made page one all over New York City. Before she even set foot on land the success of her tour was guaranteed. There would be hardly one empty seat in any hall in which she appeared from coast to coast.

She was just sixty years old when she came here. Twelve years later she died. She had a busy, exciting and phenomenally fruitful life before the tour and it continued after her return to France. But the tour was the highlight. Nothing like it had happened before or has happened since to any American writer. How and why it happened and why in truth she honestly deserved it make an unforgettable and absorbing chapter in American literature.

2 *One should always be the youngest member of the family.*
—EVERYBODY'S AUTOBIOGRAPHY

People in Oakland across the bay from San Francisco called it the old Stratton place. It was a quite special place, too. The ten-acre lot was at the corner of Thirteenth Avenue and Twenty-fifth Street. A fence surrounded the hay field, the vegetable and flower gardens, and the green lawn. In 1880, when Gertrude Stein's family moved there, the roomy, spacious house was the grandest in the neighborhood.

It had to be roomy to shelter a busy man and woman and their lively children. The man of the house, Daniel Stein, was stocky, bearded and patriarchal. He worked in the city. His business was mainly the management of streetcar lines. To reach his office he crossed the water by ferry. A band of musicians played popular tunes to while away the passengers' time from shore to shore.

The Stein family, about 1880. From left to right: Gertrude, Mrs. Stein, Bertha, Simon, Mr. Stein, and Michael. Leo reclines in the foreground.

Daniel and his wife, Amelia, or Milly, planned to have five children and no more. Or perhaps Daniel did the planning, since he was the dominant figure. They had their five but then two of them died. Faithful to their plan, they had two replacements. Of the original quintet, the survivors were Michael, the oldest, and Simon and Bertha. The two substitutes, the afterthoughts, were Leo and, youngest of all, Gertrude. Gertrude Stein grew up to be a

6

writer. For a time she was the most famous woman author, probably the most famous author, in the United States.

She used to say she felt funny about almost not being born at all. So did Leo. If the other two had not died, would there never have been Gertrude Stein's "continuous present"? Or the repetitions that stirred up so much argument about her prose? Would there never have been two Americans with the phenomenal foresight to buy the first paintings by Pablo Picasso and Henri Matisse? Would there never have been this book for me to write and you to read?

What the two children who died might have become, we cannot imagine. But they couldn't possibly have been a match for Gertrude and Leo. These last born were the creative Steins. It was natural that, as the youngest, they were drawn together a lot. Gertrude was always glad to be the youngest. She started out being pampered. She kept on being pampered in many ways all her life. She loved it that way. Fond aunts paid attention to her before they ever noticed the other youngsters. She was the one they picked up to joggle on their knee. Being the baby, she was babied. Being the youngest, she learned, "saves you a lot of bother everybody takes care of you." In one sense her life was an endless succession of obstacles to surmount and difficulties to overcome. In another sense her path was smoothed out for her. Usually there were servants. But she also had the benefit of warmer, loving care. Brother Leo squired her around. Some girls don't like big brothers. Some brothers can't stand little sisters. But for years Gertrude and Leo got along swimmingly.

Then a second Californian assumed the responsibility

7

for Gertrude Stein. This was Alice B. (B-for-Babette) Toklas. Miss Toklas lived with Gertrude Stein for the last half of the writer's life. Miss Toklas catered to Gertrude Stein's wants and ran interference for her. She put up a staunch Toklas barrier against any and all anti-Stein manifestations. There would be quite a few such manifestations, too.

Amelia Stein was sickly. Daniel hired a staff to help out. A succession of governesses started the youngsters on their ABC's. Seamstresses kept busy at the Steins' for months on end. Stores didn't stock many ready-made clothes in those years . . . 1875 to 1885 and on. The mother and girls needed new dresses and coats. Or there were adjustments to be made in the clothes Mrs. Stein ordered from Paris. Gertrude Stein would remember some seamstresses and governesses as clearly as she remembered her mother.

The person she remembered best was Leo. He was born in 1872. She was born at eight o'clock the morning of February 3, 1874. The place was Allegheny, now a part of Pittsburgh, Pennsylvania. She took a sly pleasure in pointing out that this date placed her in the most distinguished company: "In the month of February were born Washington Lincoln and I." She was six years old when the family moved to Oakland. She had a wide, high, prominent brow. Long, dark hair flowed loosely down her nape to be gathered in a bow. Her eyes were brown.

From the very start Leo paced her, as we say. She followed him into local schools. When he went to Harvard she followed again. This time she enrolled in the Harvard Annex, which by the time she graduated had changed its name to Radcliffe College. He went to Johns Hopkins in

Baltimore, she went to Johns Hopkins. He sailed off to settle in Europe and she took off after him.

This intimate brother-sister association was established in their earliest years. Gertrude would fondly recall some childhood incidents. She and Leo put up a lunch in a little cart and pulled it off to a picnic ground. They went on more distant outings to Dimond's Cañon. They rode their bicycles or traipsed around on foot.

A girl playmate who lived nearby once suggested a big party. Gertrude and Leo thought that would be fun. But the Steins were about to move to another house. All their china and silver were packed away in boxes for the moving van. The children decided to rough it. The boxes would serve as tables and chairs. Just then Michael came home. This biggest of all big brothers was a stickler for the proprieties. If they were going to have a party they must do it right. They unpacked china and silver and set the table. And they did have fun . . . until it came time for second helpings of ice cream. They had made the dessert themselves. They had put the old-fashioned freezer on the back porch and taken turns cranking it. The neighbor girl had brought along her two younger brothers. She hadn't wanted to. But her mother ordered, "Take your brothers or don't go at all." So she took them. They took the freezer. With Simon Stein's help they swiped it off the porch.

Etna Springs was some twenty miles away from their home in Oakland. Chinese coolies labored there in a silver mine. The swimming pool was filled with mineral water. Gertrude and Leo, perhaps eight or ten or twelve years old, decided to walk there. Leo took his gun. He shot two rabbits, a bird, and a squirrel. Gertrude later wished he hadn't. But at the time they were not so thoughtful as they should have been.

The day was hot. The country road was dusty. Twenty miles was a long way for a couple of youngsters. They slung the game over the barrel of the gun. Each one held an end of it to carry between them. It got pretty heavy. They threw away one rabbit. They threw away the second rabbit. They threw away the bird. A passing farmer took pity on them and offered them a lift. No thanks, they answered. They had planned to walk, and walk they would. All the way to Etna Springs? he asked. All the way, they said as if they meant it. But at last, when another farmer invited them to climb up into his wagon, they did. They explained that they had meant to walk. He joked with them: were they sure they didn't want to get down and finish their trip on foot? They were sure. Their feet in heavy, high, laced boots were sore. They rode the rest of the way. When they reached Etna Springs they thanked the farmer and gave him their squirrel.

Somehow the story spread around that the two children had walked all twenty miles in a forenoon. It grew to be a legend, or so they liked to think. They didn't deny it, either, or not at least until Gertrude Stein in college wrote a theme about it. But it was not denied around their home or in the neighborhood. They were, as they loved to imagine, a legendary pair. They had perhaps become a part of California folklore. Gertrude Stein hoped to be a part of folklore. She loved to figure in legend. She got her wish in a major way in an infinitely larger field.

3   *What is the use of being a little boy if you are growing up to be a man.*

—THE GEOGRAPHICAL HISTORY OF AMERICA

Gertrude Stein was a widely traveled little girl even before her family settled in Oakland. At that time she was six years old. There, for the first time, she heard English regularly. That was the language she would write. Or it was the language she would claim she wrote, as some like to say. Puzzled or hostile critics would accuse her of writing something else entirely: gibberish.

Before the Oakland years she had heard as much French and German as English. This was because her parents moved around not only in this country but in Europe. The father, Daniel, began his business life with three brothers in Baltimore. Then with only one brother, Solomon, he opened a clothing store in Pittsburgh, Gertrude's birthplace. He and his brother lived side by side in twin houses in Pittsburgh. Their business prospered. But Amelia Stein

11

did not get on at all with her sister-in-law. Daniel did not get on at all with his brother. With the opinionated Daniel probably the one largely to blame, the partners separated. Daniel took his whole family off to Vienna, where they visited relatives. Governesses and tutors looked after the children. Mrs. Stein and her oldest son, Michael, rode horseback in the parks. The children often saw the Emperor of Austria-Hungary, Francis Joseph, passing in his coach or walking among his people.

Leaving his family abroad, Daniel came back to the United States to enter some other line of business. This time he would go it alone without the brother he had quarreled with. He looked over the prospects in Baltimore, where he had started out, and which was also the home of Amelia Stein's family, the Keysers. Then he chose San Francisco. Mrs. Stein longed to be with her husband. To move herself and the children a little nearer, she settled briefly in Passy, a suburb of Paris. Now Gertrude, who had been hearing German, began to hear French. After a short stop in London, Amelia Stein brought her children back to the States to join Daniel in San Francisco.

Except for the relationship between Leo and Gertrude, the brothers and sisters seem not to have been demonstrably affectionate. Their association was matter-of-fact. They were perhaps more interested in each other than fond of each other. This may have led to a greater self-reliance than is commonly nurtured in growing youngsters.

Daniel was a difficult and erratic father. He was respected and admired and obeyed but perhaps not loved. The welfare of his offspring mattered a lot to him but they didn't feel that he managed their personal affairs very sensibly. Gertrude and Leo were not much fonder of him than of their mother. Interrupting his puffs on an expensive cigar, he would assure his children airily, "You're the doctor." That was supposed to put them on their own. They were then to go ahead and make their own decisions. Instead, he promptly made decisions for them. He had emphatic ideas about educating them. But his ideas kept changing radically. One year he obliged them to concentrate on music. Another year they had to exert themselves particularly in gymnastics. Once he fired the cook and informed his boys and girls that they must learn to run the house themselves. Leo claimed that he learned to cook very well. Leo also said that Gertrude, on the contrary, made a mess of the job. Perhaps he was right about himself. Certainly he was right about his young sister. She would develop the refined taste of the gourmet but the kitchen always remained an unknown and alien land to her. Cooking was never her dish.

Leo never saw his father with a book in his hands, he said. That may have been true but perhaps it gives an unfair impression of the head of the family. Daniel was alert and alive to the contemporary world. His two ideals do him credit. They were Giuseppe Garibaldi, the Italian soldier and patriot, and Louis Kossuth, the Hungarian revolutionary.

Gertrude remembered her father's lordly way of parading about the house, jingling the coins in his pocket. He was stubborn and arrogant. He laid down the law. He had a temper and exerted but little control over it. Crossed in domestic matters, he was apt to double up his fist and bang

13

on the table. Gertrude inherited a sizable streak of this temper. She was also temperamental. As a child she used to toss a coin to decide which course to follow. If it came out heads she opted for tails; if it turned up left, she did the opposite and went right.

The mother died of cancer when Gertrude was fourteen. One morning three years later Daniel Stein failed to come down to breakfast at the usual hour. The children grew more and more worried. Leo, the nimblest, climbed a ladder to peer into his father's bedroom. Daniel had died during the night.

This left the oldest son, Michael, as titular head of the clan. He had a Bachelor of Arts degree from Johns Hopkins. That could have helped prepare him for his new and heavy responsibilities. In the year of his father's death he was assistant superintendent of the Omnibus Cable Company. Daniel was vice-president. Not long afterward the young man's business acumen enabled him to consolidate the San Francisco street railways as the Market Street Railway Company. In 1895 he was appointed superintendent of the enlarged firm.

Simon was not smart enough, in Gertrude's uncharitable opinion, to earn a living at complicated work. Presumably Michael's influence helped him get a job as gripman. Cable cars rattled up and down dizzy San Francisco inclines. Simon started and stopped them on receiving the appropriate signal. It was a lifetime job and he doted on it. His pockets were always stuffed with candy, which he gave to young passengers who took his fancy.

Leo and Gertrude used to call on Michael at his office. On some special occasions he took them to a restaurant for dinner. He granted each of them a regular allowance. They spent almost every cent on books. Gertrude bought the poems of Shelley and Byron. Already at this tender age books were indispensable to her. One reason, she said, was that there "was so much to cry about in them." She read Shakespeare endlessly and tirelessly. She tried to write what she defined as a Shakespeare play. She was sailing along smoothly until she ran into trouble of her own making. A stage direction that she wrote called for a courtier to deliver some witty remarks. But she couldn't think of even one witty remark, so she abandoned the project. Thirty years later, without setting up any such artificial hurdles, she wrote a lot of plays.

On the walks with Leo, as she recalled them, they enjoyed serious discussions. It was an equal give-and-take. As Leo recalled them, she listened docilely while he lectured. From what we learn of their later lives, Leo had the correct view of this youthful relationship. He was—and remained— the pedagogue, with all the world, he hoped, as his attentive class. In those years Gertrude was marking time. Perhaps this was merely the conservative side of her nature. But she was already making her own choices. She was not abiding by the flip of a coin, she was astutely following her bent.

Did she say this early that the goal she aimed at was glory? For as far back as Leo could remember, she yearned for what the French exalt as *la gloire*. From the start, Leo said, she wanted with all her heart to be lionized. Certainly she never hesitated to admit this longing. Or did Leo merely misunderstand his talkative sister? Did she want only to be babied? No doubt each was a little right.

4 *Nothing is so intense as being alone with a book.*

—EVERYBODY'S AUTOBIOGRAPHY

The death of the second parent left the five children on their own. Now at last it was sadly true that "you're the doctor." The family was obliged to break up. Two boys, Michael and Simon, stayed in San Francisco. Simon led a happy life as a gripman. Michael earned the money to provide financial independence for them all. It is important to appreciate this generous service of his. The father had been a practical man of affairs. Michael, too, knew the value of money and how hard it is to accumulate. He might have expected his younger brothers and sisters to pitch in and help. He put his nose to the grindstone and he might have insisted that they should, too. But that was not his attitude. Instead he respected the devout commitment of Gertrude and Leo to studying, reading and writing. Their travels, their years in Paris that superficially seemed aimless and wasteful, and their purchase of paintings that other people laughed at really came out of Michael's pocket. Or they came out of the whole Stein stocking, the family stocking. Michael could have objected. On the contrary, he broadmindedly approved.

Bertha, Gertrude, and Leo went to live with their mother's relatives, the Keysers, in Baltimore. Leo wasn't at ease. He had a prickly, uncongenial nature. Games, gossip and family get-togethers didn't amuse him and he showed it inconsiderately. Anyway he soon enrolled at Harvard. Gertrude, on the other hand, was popular. She entered into family life sympathetically, she enjoyed the domestic fun. In later years she was a little brusque in dispensing with relatives. But now she was liked and she liked. The only unpleasantness was having to sleep with Bertha. At night Bertha ground her teeth.

Apparently Gertrude didn't complete all the usual years of high school. She never took to formal education. If she didn't know what she wanted, at least she knew what she didn't want. Perhaps the fault was that those were the growing-up years. She later recalled "the dark and dreadful days of adolescence." In her long novel *The Making of Americans*, a young girl says a boy "wanted her to do loving." Probably that was Gertrude Stein speaking for Gertrude Stein. She had definitely not been interested. The only boy who confessedly attracted her was still Leo.

She was hunting for a goal, a purpose. She hints at an incident that may have helped make up her mind. It seems trivial but it could have had an effect. On a downtown street in Baltimore she saw a man strike a woman with his umbrella. Why did he do that? Why did anyone behave as anyone did? The Steins were quarrelsome and it seemed other people were, too. Were there traits common to all mankind? College might provide some answers. That, she claimed, was one reason for going to the Harvard Annex, or Radcliffe. Another reason, certainly, was the desire to be near Leo. She didn't even dream at this time of any break in the little sister–big brother team. There were, however, entrance requirements, for instance Latin, which she did not have or could not meet. Even so she mailed in her application. She did not live by rules. She expected the college wouldn't stick to them, either. Despite the formal lacks she was admitted. Her application letter must have been peculiarly persuasive.

Gertrude Stein was nineteen when she went to Cambridge, Massachusetts. Would she have been a different Gertrude Stein if she had studied somewhere else? It is unlikely. But her choice was extremely fortunate or wise. It was due not merely to Leo's presence at Harvard but surely to his enthusiasm for the place. At that time probably no other faculty was a match for Harvard's. A close friend of the young girl was Thomas Whittemore of the Boston Museum of Fine Arts. He fostered her interest in painting. She studied with Josiah Royce, the idealist philosopher. She had classes with William Vaughn Moody, poet and dramatist perhaps best known for his play *The Great Divide*. She studied with the philosopher George Santayana, remembered in part for his novel *The Last Puritan*.

These were significantly creative, independent, pioneering minds. The exalted goals they had reached were an inspiration to students. The young writer-to-be undoubtedly received helpful guidance from her English teachers. Her two most important professors, however, cultivated an entirely different field: psychology. They were William James and Hugo Münsterberg.

Leo had studied with William James before his sister reached Cambridge . . . how close she followed on his heels! James was already the author of *The Principles of Psychology*, an epochal publication of 1890. As Gertrude came under his guidance, a second pioneering work was in progress, *The Will to Believe*. James's primary concern was the consciousness. What was it? According to long-cherished theory it was a static state. People regarded it as a sort of object, perhaps, something that could be hefted or measured. James emphatically rejected theorizing and favored, instead, experimenting. His criterion was the senses. Consciousness, he decided, was something that never stood still. It was a process, a changing, a never-being-the-same. He spoke of "the wonderful stream of consciousness."

This was the supreme gift to upcoming writers. Like Gertrude Stein, they would be concerned with something-going-on, with never-being-the-same, with flow, with the opposite of the static and the fixed. Dorothy Richardson wrote a "stream of consciousness" novel, *Pilgrimage*. It was twelve volumes long. Marcel Proust wrote one almost as long, *In Remembrance of Things Past*. The word *Remembrance* in this translated title may not have been quite acceptable to Gertrude Stein. She was wary of memory. Memory was frozen, it was something-that-had-gone-on. She was even wary of thinking in connection with creative work. "It is awfully easy to not be thinking not at all awfully easy," she said in *Operas and Plays*. Writing and remembering and thinking, too, had nothing in common, she believed. She might have preferred *In Search of the Past*, which is closer to Proust's original title. Yet Proust didn't go looking for it; rather, it sort of came looking for him. He didn't remember it, he re-created it.

Gertrude Stein the writer would be fascinated by the here-and-now. Thoughts about yesterday were extraneous. They blotted out awareness of today. When she wrote her major novel, *The Making of Americans*, she let it flow on for more than nine hundred pages, or more than half a million words. Stream-of-consciousness authors were not short-winded. What they wrote was not figured out, not remembered, planned or plotted. It sort of bubbled up. Some painters created in the same way. The brush wandered along on its own, it was not pushed or directed. A painter might pour paint on a canvas straight out of a bucket. Or he stood back and splashed the colors on. Then he framed it and gave it a title and called it art. It was art, too. Some composers followed the same method, or lack of method. They picked sounds out of surrounding life and ran them together. Gertrude Stein's goal, by her definition in *What Are Masterpieces*, was a "continuous present." This began right in Cambridge in William James's class. He told her always to keep an open mind. Take nothing for granted, he said. At the same time she was to be utterly aware. There is a phrase from an old song, "I don't know where I'm going but I'm on my way." Gertrude Stein once quoted it. Her writing didn't know where it was going but it was on its way.

A river is never the same, a Greek philosopher argued. It changes, since the water in the river continuously changes. James propounded a related idea: consciousness is never the same; it, too, changes. There cannot, for instance, be any repetition. You say a thing. A minute later you say exactly the same thing again. It is not the same, however. The second time it comes out of a different you . . . the water has flowed on. It arises out of a developing, altered consciousness. It is like a cloudy sky, always cloudy but never the same clouds. So Gertrude Stein said she repeated in her writings. She also said she did not repeat. She was right both times.

Münsterberg was the laboratory psychologist. He performed the experimenting which, James felt, should replace theorizing. He sought the tangible, demonstrable, physical measurements of the nature of consciousness. Gertrude Stein was an outstanding follower of his teaching. He told her, "You were to me the ideal student." This praise presumably made it possible for her to enter James's advanced classes, for which she normally would not have been eligible. She was as little interested in theory as James. A thing must pass the obvious, discernible, plain-as-your-nose test of the senses.

The extracurricular life in Cambridge was as novel and strange as the classwork. It was Gertrude Stein's first extended experience away from home and relatives. Like most of her classmates, she rented a room in a boardinghouse.

She arrived with a heavy load of books. Unlike many other girls, she brought very few clothes. She was never fashion-conscious. For this her new friends made fun of her. One of them snitched an old hat she constantly wore and destroyed it. But as she had been popular with Baltimore cousins and aunts and uncles, she was also popular with fellow students. She liked boys as well as girls. Boys liked her, too, though they appear to have liked her passively. Gertrude and her friends went on long walks. They took bicycle trips. They went boating. Gertrude Stein was secretary of the Philosophical Club. She heard a lot of opera, too, especially Wagner. Nearby Boston offered more performances than Baltimore or San Francisco. Music, however, would not matter much to her creatively. The question of sound and resonance would not enter into her choice of words.

She didn't see as much of Leo as she had expected to. Fresh preoccupations loosened the old ties. With Münsterberg and James as mentors, she worked on elaborate experiments. The most significant ones were carried out in association with a graduate student, Leon Solomons. Solomons became her closest college friend. Together they experimented with colors and sounds. But their particular field was words, so they turned inevitably to writing. Could one write automatically? Automatic writing may be compared to the use of a planchette on a Ouija board. The board has letters, the planchette has a pointed end. You let your mind go blank. Your fingertips rest lightly on the planchette. You wait to see whether of its own volition it will slide around here and there and form words. Solomons and his young partner tried it. They were faithfully following James's advice to take nothing for granted, to find out for themselves. They composed a paper, "Normal Motor Automatism." It was published in 1896 in the *Psychological Review*. Both of them signed it. Later Gertrude Stein did an experiment all her own. Her findings, entitled "Cultivated Motor Automatism," were published under her name alone in the same review.

These were Gertrude Stein's first appearances in print. But there are two other important aspects to the laboratory work. One is that it was done in the area of automatic writing. Years later this would cause some embarrassing moments. Critics who didn't understand her or didn't like her, or both, would recall these experiments and connect them damagingly with her mature writing. They would accuse her of automatic—that is, mindless—writing, and add that she was mindless herself. To be sure there were superficial resemblances, especially in the flow of disconnected words, between Gertrude Stein's mature work and work produced by automatic writing. But she denied that any of her writing was automatic. The first of the two youthful papers expressed Solomons' views rather than her own, she explained. In her defense she declared emphatically, "I had no results there was no automatic writing . . . never any words or anything that could be called automatic writing." And she added, "I concluded that there is no such thing as automatic writing among the people as one knows them." There is no reason to doubt this. She wrote consciously and, as someone has said, she should be read consciously.

The other important aspect of her laboratory work is a

23

consequence of her second major experiment. To carry it out she had the cooperation of some forty fellow students. Half of them were Harvard boys, half were Radcliffe girls. She used them primarily on a Münsterberg project. But their important contribution was to her knowledge of people. It occurred to her that, though they all had some differences, they all had some traits in common. Some basic and fundamental things were repeated in them . . . as there would be repetitions in her prose. She made charts and diagrams of them. She believed she could make outlines that encompassed the entire human race. She grouped her subjects, her guinea pigs, according to their "bottom nature," as she said. For instance, some people were "independent dependents" and others were "dependent independents." Most novelists make notes. Gertrude Stein's notes were more general and less specific. Yet they were an essential tool when she began *The Making of Americans*.

William James was her idol. She praised him extravagantly in a paper composed for one of her classes: "A man he is who has lived sympathetically not alone all thought but all life. He stands firmly, nobly for the dignity of man. . . . He has thought and lived many years and at last says with a voice of authority, if life does not mean this, I don't know what it means." This was infinitely more than a schoolgirl's crush. This was the tribute of a humble but independent and ardent mind. James, in return, specially appreciated her talent. Her course with him wound up in an examination. The long, tiring business required her to sit at a desk and scribble out what answers she could. Her classmates did their duty. She rebelled. She simply wrote a note to her teacher on her paper: "Dear Professor James, I am so sorry but really I do not feel a bit like an examination paper in philosophy today." Then she turned this in and walked out of the hall. James promptly mailed her a postcard: "Dear Miss Stein: I understand perfectly how you feel I often feel like that myself." He gave her the highest mark in his class.

In these college years Gertrude Stein had left the familiar circle of her family. She had ventured into the outside world. It is always a critical time for youth. But this was a test she did not shirk, a test that she passed easily. Teachers and fellow students and the whole Radcliffe ambiance helped to mold her.

But the most important record we have from this future writer was the writing she did at Radcliffe. In 1894 and 1895 numerous English themes were required of her. She was twenty and twenty-one years old. The stories and articles are a few paragraphs long or amount to a few pages. The subjects are a ghost, a trip to the opera, a suitor, the family, a family quarrel. One character is a girl lonely and motherless, much like the young author. In one ambitious tale two youngsters—Harry, thirteen, and the girl narrator, eleven—take a long walk into the mountains. The day is hot, they kick up dust along the country road. At last a kind farmer gives them a lift. But they make believe they had possessed the stamina to walk every step of the way. Afterward they like to think this event grew into a legend. This was, of course, the story of Leo and Gertrude, two years his junior, and their trek to Etna Springs.

Teachers complained justifiably about Gertrude's grammar and her spelling. She had to rewrite some themes. It was the last rewriting she ever did, too. But her teachers were impressed. They liked the ideas and the emotions expressed by this novice.

She should have clung to this praise and cherished it. She would have to wait twenty or thirty discouraging years before anyone else in an official capacity admitted he liked her writing.

5 *You don't know what it is to be bored.*
—THE AUTOBIOGRAPHY OF ALICE B. TOKLAS

Gertrude Stein did not receive her Radcliffe degree at the same time as her classmates. She still had to make up the missing Latin credit. In the fall of 1897, however, she was admitted to Johns Hopkins Medical School. Something about her did not brook obstacles. She pushed through doors closed to other people. She had managed to enter the Harvard Annex though she lacked some requirements. Now she enrolled in Johns Hopkins without even a preliminary degree. But by dint of tutoring in Latin she was awarded her A.B. in 1898.

She still liked Baltimore. Now twenty-three years old, she no longer lived with her mother's relatives. She and Leo shared an apartment. It was near the Johns Hopkins campus, though in a somewhat shabby neighborhood. When Leo left she stayed on alone. A servant tended to her

27

Gertrude Stein at Johns Hopkins.

domestic wants. Negro voices, she found, had a quality lacking in white voices; they were mellow and soothing. She enjoyed the balmy air. She liked the sun and used to sit, she said, staring into it open-eyed.

Sir William Osler, as distinguished as her Harvard professors, was the star on the Johns Hopkins faculty. By chance he was one of those rare scientists who could write well. Much of Gertrude Stein's work the first two years was in laboratories. It was the sort of activity she had enjoyed at Harvard and she liked it here, too. She forgot the warnings of some well-meaning friends. One said she should never have entered college, any college. Woman's place was in the home. It is an argument occasionally heard today and no more valid now than then. Another friend pointed out that medical schools did not welcome women. And in fact they did not. Some students at Johns Hopkins used to tease the women. They would ask, "Are you doctors or are you ladies?" The implication was that they couldn't be both. This sort of mild hazing did not divert Gertrude Stein from her course. Perhaps, indeed, it helped prepare her for the difficulties that would hamper her as a writer. Opposition stiffened her determination. They didn't want her in Johns Hopkins? Then she'd stick it out. They wouldn't read her writing? Then she'd give them more and more of it. She might never have scored her triumphs if her path had been smooth and clear.

A certain cocksureness about her irked some of her professors. Thanks to her successes at Radcliffe, she was aware that she possessed scholarly qualifications of a special sort. She intended to have them recognized. Besides, a lazy streak ran through her. It looked all the broader to the carping observer because it was her nature not to rush. Things must simmer. She believed in slow and sure . . . sure probably and slow certainly. To make matters worse,

29

she began to wonder whether she really did need this medical education. William James had recommended it, since he required a medical degree for his work in psychology. But would she continue in the field of psychology? A little medical know-how might carry her as far in this direction as she would ever care to go.

The first two years at Johns Hopkins went well enough. But the last two did not. They included some field work. She helped deliver babies born to indigent families. She did not enjoy that part of the course in obstetrics. Harvard gave her a degree a year late. Johns Hopkins gave her no degree at all. By her own account most of the faculty approved of her work in the laboratory and in class. But one obstinate professor wanted something more from her than vague, general, abstract signs of intelligence. He wanted her to be competent and informed about his subject. She flunked his final examination and he kept her from getting a degree. But he assured her she could get it by making up her work that summer. No thanks, she replied. She meant the thanks, too. She told him she welcomed this excuse to bow out of medicine for good. She'd had enough. His refusal of a passing mark made her decision easier.

This was the version she supplied some twenty years later. Understandably she was inclined to put as good a face on this situation as possible. Understandably also, her memory might have slipped in two long decades. Though her account contains some truth, the main facts are different. She failed in several courses. One teacher accused her of untidy and careless laboratory techniques. According to one rumor she in fact did precious little work at all. Evidently family and friends foresaw this dismal outcome. Leo, in

Europe, wrote in mild alarm that he hoped she wouldn't leave a blot on the Stein name. A New York friend urged her to carry on in the name of her sex. She should prove she could accomplish what she had set out to. Her reply was, "You don't know what it is to be bored."

She had had more than enough of formal education. She never stopped learning, she never stopped studying. From now on, however, she chose her own reading and mapped out her own courses. She might have developed into a fine science writer—a person always in short supply. She did not give up science, or writing. But she made her own unique demands on them. The scientific approach to writing absorbed her. If she rarely had a conventional story to tell, she invariably had an unconventional way of telling it. People interested her for her own sake, not for theirs.

What Gertrude Stein wanted was not just to stop what she was doing. She wanted to start something else. She had the wanderlust. Some vacation months had been spent in San Francisco. Some summers had been spent with Leo in Europe. He was way ahead: he had already sailed around the world. She determined to catch up. The bond with Johns Hopkins now definitely severed, she took off for Italy.

There the brother and sister vagabonded through old towns, looked at old paintings, and admired churches and palaces. They passed some time at I Tatti, home of the celebrated art connoisseur Bernard Berenson, also a Harvard alumnus. In the fall the Steins traveled to England. For a time they occupied a cottage in the Lake District. They planned to live during the winter in London and rented rooms in Bloomsbury Square. This fermenting cultural center was handy to the British Museum. In its great domed Reading Room Gertrude Stein sat for hours and days. She discovered the novelist Anthony Trollope, who always remained a favorite. She read the essayist Walter Pater.

There was some significant socializing. The Berensons, also in England at the moment, entertained Leo and Gertrude. The two travelers met the Berensons' in-laws: Bertrand Russell, the mathematician and philosopher, and Mrs. Russell. They met Israel Zangwill, the Jewish writer. Unknown young Americans today don't fly off to England to be welcomed by major creative personages there. They didn't sixty or seventy years ago, either. So there must have been something specially attractive about this couple. In appearance and manner they were not particularly prepossessing, it must be admitted. Leo was a bit stiff, a bit aggressive. His sister, only five feet two inches tall, weighed over two hundred pounds at that time. Theirs was the triumph of mind over matter. They could hold a person's attention. They used their heads. Obviously they were an exceptionally cultured pair.

For some reason Gertrude Stein was not happy in London. Perhaps the weather oppressed her. She had been used to the sunny warmth of Baltimore. Her distinguished acquaintances could not hold her, nor could Leo himself. She returned to the United States. For several months she and two other women about her age lived in New York. They shared an apartment way uptown with a view over the Hudson River. Here Gertrude Stein began seriously to write. The life in Baltimore and the life in New York inspired her to get to work. She was on her way.

6 Those who create things do not need adventure.

—WHAT ARE MASTERPIECES

As we shall see, Leo had found an apartment in Paris on the Left Bank. In 1903 Gertrude joined him there. It was her home for thirty-five years. She did not set foot in the United States again for more than thirty years. She started her life in Paris by turning diligently and purposefully to writing. That was the way she ended her life there, too.

Her first major work, begun in New York, was brought to a finish in her new home. The title she gave it was *Q. E. D.* (The initials stand for the familiar *quod erat demonstrandum*, borrowed from solutions for geometry problems.) It is the story of, or it is a story about, Adele. The author-narrator tells of her real experiences, her imagined experiences, and the thoughts that occurred to her while she lived with two other women. There is autobiographical material. Some things that take place took place

33

and some did not. The essence of the book is all that pours through Gertrude Stein's lively, inquiring mind.

Among Adele and the two women whom she joins there is ardent rivalry for the affection of one for another. How do they feel about living together? What do they do about it? Do their desires conflict with the beliefs they hold? This was what Gertrude Stein wrote about. The subject was very old, as old as men and women. But it was a subject rarely treated in fiction. Gertrude Stein, when she finished it, didn't dream it could ever be published. It was put away and forgotten for years. Then Gertrude Stein happened to come across it. A few friends read it and very much approved. Even so, it did not appear in print until after her death. Then the title was changed to *Things As They Are*. There were no stylistic innovations. The writing was nineteenth century, not twentieth. It was not the sort of prose to draw critical attention. Yet it was the Stein manner of thinking . . . free, bold, frank. In short, Gertrude Stein had not yet fully blossomed into Gertrude Stein.

That happened only in her next book, *Three Lives*. There had been three parts to *Things As They Are*. Now there were three separate novellas under one title but unified by a single mood and theme. The first work of fiction had a vague base in Gertrude Stein's life in uptown New York. The second was allied closely to her years in Baltimore. Her home there was in a commonplace neighborhood. There is something commonplace about her trio of subjects, three lower-class women, two white and one black. They are servants or housekeepers of menial status. The stories are bleak and undramatic. People talk and talk and talk or they are talked to and talked about. Then it's all over.

Gertrude Stein's own life ran along pretty much on an even keel year after year, decade after decade. To be sure, she lived through two calamitous world wars, most of the time in a country tragically involved in them. During the first she and her friend Miss Toklas narrowly escaped some dangers, and during the second they escaped some situations that were still worse. Yet on the whole they experienced both wars passively. There were no derring-do adventures, no hairbreadth brushes with death. Other creative workers have paid a heavy price merely to exist in our often unsympathetic and hostile world. The painter Paul Gauguin broke up his family and fled to a shoddy Bohemian existence on the romantic island of Tahiti. Another artist, Vincent van Gogh, sliced off an ear in a fit of passion. Gertrude Stein's longtime friend and admirer, the novelist Ernest Hemingway, knew violence firsthand. In World War I he was wounded. As a big-game hunter he suffered severe injuries. Eventually he committed suicide. But major crises stayed well away from the Stein path. Gertrude Stein just sat at her desk and ran her great sprawling handwriting over reams of paper. She walked her dog, entertained friends, argued, reasoned, listened, talked and mulled over life and its meaning. Of course she was swayed by intense and passionate sentiments. She had a temper. But in a way she took shelter in an ivory tower. She remained regally aloof from the tumult of the world.

Partly as a consequence of this drastic isolation, her fiction is uneventful. She wrote what she knew and what she observed; she was autobiographical. If she did not put much action in her pages, it was to a degree because she was not interested in action. If she was not interested, it was because action had not figured significantly in her personal experience. She did not have at hand, for instance, the material for much conventional plotting. What she knew and dreamed of and wrote didn't develop naturally or smoothly into the usual climax. If her characters made love or quarreled, they did so offstage. Her concern was the springs of action. It was a person's being, not at all his doing, that she proposed to pin down on paper. "I believe I do not like anything that happens," she wrote in *The Geographical History of America.*

Three Lives is this kind of story. Nothing quite like it had been attempted before. It grew directly out of Gertrude Stein's life in her Baltimore apartment. The epigraph is a quotation credited to a French moralist, Jules Laforgue: "So I am an unfortunate man and it's not my fault nor the fault of life." Gertrude Stein's three characters could have uttered a lament in almost the same words: "So I am an unfortunate woman. . . ."

The scene common to the stories is "Bridgepoint," the name she used for Baltimore in the book. The first is about "The Good Anna," Anna Federner, a servant. The third is about "The Gentle Lena," who endures the extremes of a drab and humdrum existence. She is engaged to Herman Kreder. That pleases her. It cannot be said to delight her, for emotions here do not rise above calm and restrained levels. It does not particularly please Herman. On the wedding day he stands her up at church. She did not go into ecstasies at the engagement. She does not sink into despair at being left crudely in the lurch. Herman's mother takes Lena's part. She drags her reluctant son to the altar and the two at last are married. They live together until Lena's death at the birth of her fourth child. She is an unfortunate woman and it isn't her fault.

The outstanding story is the central one and the longest, "Melanctha." The subtitle is, "Each One As She May." Melanctha is a Negro. Like Anna and Lena, she was modeled on someone Gertrude Stein had known. Like the others, she was to be drawn in general outline from the elaborate charts plotted at Radcliffe and covering in theory all possible types of human beings. In the author's mind she was Everywoman just as the author conceived of her male characters as Everyman. Melanctha Herbert is led into bad company by the beguilement of her friends Rose Johnson and Jane Harden. Then for most of the story she is courted, now successfully and now not, by a doctor, Jeff Campbell.

There are numerous strings of adjectives. Rose, for instance, is "tall, well built, sullen, stupid, childlike, good looking." These sound like adjectives culled from the charts of the author's student years. There are also repetitions which aroused storms of criticism as well as paeans of praise. The repetitions are not merely of words but on occasion of events. Rose, for example, says Melanctha never comes to see her any more. Melanctha, in turn, says she never goes to see Rose any more. You hear it from both sides. The fact is tied down and made unmistakable. It is also made unforgettable. The two versions belong. With only one, you learn only one half of the truth. In *The Making of Americans* Gertrude Stein would eloquently defend "the loving there is in me for repeating."

One after another Melanctha entertains a lot of men friends. Thanks to Rose she has acquired the questionable habit of variety and change. Her wavering, her instability and her infidelities drive the unhappy Jeff to complain, "I certainly know now really, how I don't know anything sure at all about you, Melanctha." He keeps at her, she keeps at him. He tries to pin her down. She will see him, she will not see him. By an endless succession of one step forward and two steps back and then two steps forward and one step back, they draw together and they separate. It is a classic courtship and a classic rejection.

Melanctha's trouble is described succinctly. Many people in and out of books suffer from it: "Melanctha had not found it easy with herself to make her wants and what she had, agree." It's another way of saying that she couldn't make both ends meet . . . moral, emotional, financial, social ends. It is unfolded slyly word by word, it comes in short quiet breaths not in great gasps. There are no slambang hair-raising scenes but only understatement piled on understatement. Critics say of a book they like that they can't put it down. You can put this down. But you can't keep from picking it up again. It stays with you. It is an abstraction of dramatic values. Once you venture within the magic Melanctha circle, you are hooked.

"Melanctha" is one of the masterpieces of twentieth-century literature. Yet to get it and the two companion stories published, Gertrude Stein had to pay the printer herself. We subscribe to the general notion that really superior writing makes its own way. Perhaps it does, eventually. But at the start there are exceptions. Marcel Proust dug into his pocket to launch his great literary career. James Joyce at first did not strike any commercial publisher as a worthwhile proposition. Gertrude Stein was not alone in having to combat the indifference of commerce.

Some Negroes felt that there was a touch of condescension in "Melanctha." Others regarded it as a sincere tribute to their race. Novelist Richard Wright, as critical of whites as any of his fellow blacks, praised it highly. He thought Gertrude Stein was the first white writer really to do justice to the Negro, his place, his wants, his frustrations, his "bottom nature." The poet James Weldon Johnson definitely approved.

All three stories are stark and simple. They are absolutely devoid of decoration or ornament. Undramatic people turn into drama. You are bound up with the fate of these hapless women. What doesn't interest us in other writers does interest us here. Gertrude Stein has more or less turned the craft of fiction inside out. The dull, ordinary, and commonplace hold our unflagging attention. The author claimed she intended deliberately to put the commonplace in her writing. This is precisely what other authors strive to keep out. In her hands the commonplace grows exciting. It begins to breathe fire. The stories drone along. But this very drone and hum exert an irresistible magnetism. We are hypnotized. She has no rabbit up her sleeve yet the rabbit is produced before our startled eyes.

When you read Gertrude Stein you rarely need a dictionary. Your everyday, workaday vocabulary is hers, too. It is grammar-school, or at the most junior-high, English. In this it is a marked contrast to the fiction of her contemporary James Joyce. To read his *Ulysses* or *Finnegans Wake* you must resort to dictionaries in several languages, dead as well as living. Gertrude Stein's words are short and often monosyllabic. If you don't notice what is said the first time it is quite certain to be said again. And then it is said still again. The author takes a theme as a composer does. But instead of developing it she often seems to be playing it over and over again. Other writing is the hare; this writing is the tortoise. It is a succession of participles and gerunds. As Gertrude Stein wrote in *The Making of Americans*, "There is now then coming to be an ending of the beginning of the Hersland family." Or as we read later, "This is then now to be a little description of loving repeating being in one . . . This is then a beginning of the way of knowing." This is a present that goes on and on. It is not thought but thinking, not deed but doing, not talk but talking. Gertrude Stein is always aiming to be persuading you to be understanding that you are reading it at the exact moment when it is being happening.

She did not write in a vacuum. She had read and studied other authors, for instance Henry James. She was sensitive to the ferment in the cultural world just after the dawn of the new century. Two encounters had a particular influence on her epochal *Three Lives*. One was with a book, the other with a painting. Both were French.

Leo's enthusiasm for the French novelist Gustave Flaubert was communicated to his sister. She started a translation of a Flaubert volume called *Three Stories*. A girl in one of them, Félicité, was as uninspiring and commonplace as the women in *Three Lives*. There is little in Gertrude Stein's work that resembles Flaubert's kind of heightened realism. Nevertheless he had set a precedent of sorts. It must have encouraged her to plunge ahead on her own path.

Again it was Leo who introduced her to the painting, *Portrait of Madame Cézanne*. This work by Paul Cézanne hung on the wall above the massive table on which Gertrude Stein wrote. Madame Cézanne is sitting in a chair facing to the right. One arm is bent at the elbow and the forearm lies across her waist. The dominant colors are red and green. We can imagine Gertrude Stein intent on her work but uncannily conscious of her company, her guest, her tutor. It was less the sitter than the painter that concerned her. Paul Cézanne worked much as Gertrude Stein worked. His brushstrokes may be likened to her pen strokes. His study of a woman was a counterpart of her study of a woman. Both creative workers drove toward the same goal. Both were interested in the simple, the plain, the unexceptionable. Neither sought a climax. Each one thought every single word or every spot of paint as important as the next word or the next spot of paint.

Three Lives is not just about people, and the Cézanne *Portrait* is not just about a woman. Each is a work of art and each has a life and an existence of its own. Each is an entity. As Gertrude Stein would say, to quote from *The*

Paul Cézanne's *Portrait of Madame Cézanne* (right) hung above the work table at 27 rue de Fleurus.

Making of Americans, each one is a "whole one." The immediate influences shaping and guiding the young American writer were French. The long-term influences, like the subject matter, were through-and-through American. Looming large in the background was William James's imperative: investigate, probe, be yourself.

7 *America is my country.*

Henry James lived in England for years. He acknowledged his indebtedness to his adopted land by becoming a
British citizen just before his death in 1916. James Joyce,
leaving Ireland early, made the Continent his permanent
home. Gertrude Stein, expatriate for more than half her
life, nevertheless remained an American, heart and soul.
Joyce tried to get Ireland out of his blood but he could
never get it out of his books. Gertrude Stein would have
hated to get America out of her blood and she never did.
It stayed with her and with her writing to the last.

The pure and intense Americanism of this woman who
obstinately remained away from America inspired numerous observations. Miss Toklas remarked, "I did not realize
then on first acquaintance how completely and entirely
American was Gertrude Stein." Sherwood Anderson wrote

to Gertrude Stein, "you would be surprised to know just how altogether American I found you." According to the poet Lloyd Frankenberg, she was "one of the most patriotic of the expatriates." Biographer Elizabeth Sprigge, a Londoner, called Gertrude Stein "so American." Bernard Faÿ, the French historian, was the most emphatic: "She is more interested in America, more anxious to understand, express, describe, and give to her readers the real America than any other American writer."

She never tried so hard to do just that as in her long novel *The Making of Americans*. Ernest Hemingway wrote about his fellow countrymen, too, though his settings were often glamorously foreign. Henry James took Americans for his subjects. Gertrude Stein wrote about Americans exhaustively. She was never homesick. She was a true cosmopolitan. But of all her loyalties, none was more constant than that to the United States. Though the long novel was written in Paris, it is exclusively American in subject, spirit, method, purpose. Her characters are grounded in her native soil. "There is the American flag and it looks good," a girl exclaims in *Things As They Are*. It looked good to Gertrude Stein all her life.

The Making of Americans was her *magnum opus*. At least so she judged and so do the major critics. It would wait years for publication. When it finally appeared in 1925 there was a moment's hesitation on the author's part. Just this once she faltered. Should it be cut, or perhaps discreetly trimmed? An abridgment published in 1934 was "edited and shortened" by Bernard Faÿ. He performed a signal service for the American writer . . . though in the end he would be immeasurably more in her debt than she was in his. The full-length version is the purer Stein. To cut is to weaken. The novel needs the bulk. It is persistent, it is almost ruthless in the way it drives on and on. Cut it and you diminish the thrust and momentum. You are meant to read this, it might be said, even if it kills you. Once you are committed to Stein, however, you will read it and it won't kill you after all.

With *The Hersland Family* as subtitle and Bridgepoint again standing for Baltimore, Gossols now becomes Gertrude Stein's substitute for Oakland. She doesn't make up these names, she adapts them. Picasso for instance, her Spanish painter friend, had spent a summer in Gozols in his native land. Hersland is a variant of Hirschland, the name of relatives.

"It has always seemed to me a rare privilege, this, of being an American," says the narrator of this involved epic. She proceeds to dig and dig into the "bottom nature" of Americans. It is her family she writes about specifically. Her intention is to embrace all her country and all her countrymen.

It's hard to tell the story of *The Making of Americans*. That is not because it is obscure or unclear. Gertrude Stein still clung to rudimentary punctuation in this novel. Practically every sentence reveals its meaning at first glance. But there is precious little story to tell. To be sure, there are people. They live in a big house set in a ten-acre lot . . . so we are told again and again. Fields and orchards surround them. We recognize the old Stratton place in Oakland.

Youngsters go bicycling. There are seamstresses and governesses.

There was occasional sharp give-and-take among the members of the Stein family. Little of that enters into this work of fiction. The people are clearly capable of quarrel and dissent. But they stop short of it though they have plenty of space in which to go the limit. In addition to material recognizably true to the Stein life, some is made up. A grandfather's trade is butchering, though apparently neither the Stein nor the Keyser forebears included a butcher. Grandfather, son and grandson bear the same name, David. This fictional device suggests continuity.

What is told is all-inclusive. There is no selectivity, no discrimination, no elimination. It all pours out on paper. Gertrude Stein gives us the complete impression inch by inch, as in a Cézanne painting. One inch counts as much as every other inch, there are no highlights. Yet despite the formless flood of description and information, there is method in the telling. To begin with, we learn the various classifications in which human beings may be grouped. We are told which ones the characters do not fit into. At last the spaces on the charts where they do belong are revealed. The novel is exhaustive, it is thorough. It considers all the possibilities. Then it rejects them one after another and thus arrives at the unarguable, undeniable fundamentals. In theological schools ministers used to be taught to repeat their message if they wanted the congregation to get it. Three times was a recommended dosage. Gertrude Stein never attended a theological school. But she told things three times, even three times three times. Until you get used to it, you may pull back. Not for me, you say warily. But it is catching.

"Sometime there will be written a long book that is a real history of every one who ever were or are or will be living, from their beginning to their ending," we read. In effect this is that. It starts at the domestic hearth and spreads out far. Two dressmakers are identified, Lillian Rosenhagen and Mary Maxworthing, and there are friends named Shilling. One governess, Madeleine Wyman, is Mrs. Hersland's favorite. Mrs. Hersland, perhaps like Amelia Stein, is among the least positive of the characters. She stays mainly in a quiet backwater. The tastes and interests of others in her family interest her only slightly. In the older generation it is the men who matter. "The little mother was not very important to them," we are told. The little mother was not very important, either, to Gertrude and Leo. Hersland himself is a bossy extrovert. He has directions and instructions to pass out to everyone. He never says or even thinks, "You're the doctor." In the Hersland family he *is* the doctor. You'd like to get thin, get fat? Do it this way, he orders. He volunteers advice to everybody.

The daughter, Martha Hersland, bears some resemblance to Gertrude Stein. One implication is that she was not overly popular with playmates. (Perhaps this resulted from the concentration of her interest on Leo or perhaps this was the cause of it.) On an occasional evening Martha is allowed to play away from home. But then her busybody father forbids this. Then he immediately forgets about it, and later he issues his order again. Or he finds fault with

48

Martha's brother . . . perhaps in the role of Michael . . . for not watching over his adolescent sister more carefully.

Martha enrolling in college makes the acquaintance of Phillip Redfern. Phillip is the fictional counterpart of Leon Solomons, Gertrude Stein's friend at Harvard. Solomons, in fact, died early, before *The Making of Americans* was written. Apparently Gertrude never saw him after they left Cambridge. In the novel, however, Martha becomes Phillip's wife. She is pictured as young, blond, and good-looking. Gertrude Stein was indeed young but the rest is pardonable make-believe. She was brunette not blond. She was not in any popular or superficial sense good-looking in her teens or early twenties. In advanced life she was impressively, monumentally handsome. At the time Martha-Gertrude married Phillip-Leon, a boy would not have been tempted to whistle at her. After Phillip marries, he accepts a teaching position. He falls in love with another faculty member and leaves Martha in the lurch . . . this reminds us of Herman's desertion of Lena in *Three Lives*. When Phillip dies, Martha goes back to live with her father.

This odd episode does contain quite probable autobiographical associations. It occurs unexpectedly in the midst of the massive novel. The short passage is disconcertingly close to conventional fiction. The ordinary novelist uses run-of-the-mill incidents like this in his ordinary stories. Here is action. Young people marry, disagree and die all in so many words and right before your eyes. Old-fashioned words are employed in an old-fashioned treatment of an old-fashioned situation. The thing you missed at first in Gertrude Stein you suddenly get. And getting it comes as a shock. It makes you wonder why you were bothered at missing it. It doesn't belong. In the context of the real Stein it does not ring true. By the time you have read this far you are a committed Steinian. You now take in stride her avant-garde style. This traditional passage sticks up in the middle of it all like a sore thumb. The Stein manner may be boring you but it is convincing you. You have somehow become mesmerized and you resent being un-mesmerized. You don't want to be brought back to the old reality. When the hypnotist snaps his fingers and pulls you back, you wish he hadn't.

It is a strange and significant reading experience. You didn't like the book when you started because it was so different. Before long this new, different, revolutionary manner has won you over. The proof of it is that the relapse into the old and traditional disturbs you. The novelist introduced this episode to parallel an emotional crisis in her own life. She didn't put it in to test you. But one effect is to provide the test and it is an instructive one. It reminds us how easy it is to become used to change.

"Every word I am ever using in writing has for me very existing being. Using a word I have not yet been using in my writing is to me very difficult and a peculiar feeling." So says Gertrude the narrator. It is her emphasis on her distrust of out-of-the-ordinary words. Incidentally it amounts to a defense of a simplicity approaching Basic English. She hopes you find in her words the same excitement she does. But she is not sure there is a you. This was a long book to write without ever for so much as a minute being sure anyone would read it. On and off she must have been working on it from her first year in Paris, 1903, to 1911; her main effort was 1906 to 1908. "Bear it in your mind my reader," she apostrophizes. But at once she succumbs to her doubts and adds ruefully, "... but truly I never feel it that there ever can be for me any such a creature." Yet in these same pages she manages with no difficulty at all to regain her self-confidence. The truth is that it rarely failed her. She refers to herself as "a great author." She justifies the author's snail-like progress with the claim, "Knowing real being in men and women is a very slow proceeding." She can't help herself. She must go it her own way. She didn't need William James to reassure her on this score. Every writer worth his salt in every clime and every age has gone it his own way, too.

Lots of phrases, sentences and paragraphs in the later Stein writing are eminently quotable. They have indeed been quoted everywhere, from student seminars to the halls of Congress. *The Making of Americans* contains a few such passages but they do not lift out easily. The novel is tightly knit. The amputation of one section, you find, pulls out too many loose threads with it. Having to explain the threads spoils the quotation. But one passage has been quoted often. It has to do with a stubborn and temperamental child, Martha Hersland, or Gertrude Stein. It also has to do with an umbrella. It demonstrates the "very slow proceeding" by which this author advanced. It also shows how effective her method, style and approach were. The style fits the subject perfectly. It is not possible to tell this story any better than it is told here; and what is told and how it is told are equally fascinating. It is full also of the repeating for which there was in Gertrude Stein so much "loving":

> This one, and the one I am now beginning describing is Martha Hersland and this is a little story of the acting in her of her being in her very young living, this one was a very little one then and she was running and she was in the street and it was a muddy one and she had an umbrella that she was dragging and she was crying. "I will throw the umbrella in the mud," she was saying, she was very little then, she was just beginning her schooling, "I will throw the umbrella in the mud," she said and no one was near her and she was dragging the umbrella and bitterness possessed her, "I will throw the umbrella in the mud," she was saying and nobody heard her, the others had run ahead to get home and they had left her "I will throw the umbrella in the mud," and there was desperate anger in her; "I have throwed the umbrella in the mud," burst from her, she had thrown the umbrella in the mud and that was the end of it all in her. She had thrown the umbrella in the mud and no one had heard her as it burst from her. "I have throwed the umbrella in the mud," it was the end of it all to her.

This is a girl in a temper. She is described with spice and tang. It is a legitimate flare-up. There are only four sentences. There are still the helpful commas and quotation marks, or some of them. We find some grammatical concessions which she will refuse to make later. At this crucial period she could not bring herself to break wholly with precedent. She could not be sure just how much she should comply with convention in order to speak her mind and have herself heeded. The whole idea of the long novel was apt to shock the everyday reader. She was willing to yield on details to alienate as few as possible. She was not burning all her bridges.

There is unlikely to be any run on this book in the libraries. Just the same it is an essential work in the history of our fiction. Anyone seriously concerned with the literature of our time must take it into account. No one will make a movie out of it. Yet that is not a relevant criticism. You do not necessarily enjoy the past in this or that aspect. Yet without it the present would have been different. *The Making of Americans* is a measure of the past and the present and the future; it's a landmark.

We must remember that Gertrude Stein kept referring to this not as story but as history. So her book opens doors. It adds another splendid dimension to the phenomenal versatility of the novel.

8 *It is the only reproduction of me which is always I, for me.*

—PICASSO

Three Lives and *The Making of Americans* were written at 27 rue de Fleurus. This short street branches off from the boulevard Raspail in the direction of the far end of the Luxembourg Gardens. It was and is a middle-class residential area. Not one of the city's oldest sections, it is close nevertheless to the two-thousand-year-old heart of Paris. It is on the edge of the Latin Quarter, where artists and writers congregate, where thousands of students attend the Sorbonne, the French university. Only a few minutes away are two cafés, the Dôme and the Rotonde, that were patronized by many of Gertrude Stein's friends—though she was never a café-goer herself.

Leo chose the apartment on the rue de Fleurus and invited his sister to join him. A friend of his had done a thorough job of apartment-hunting for himself, and had picked the one that suited him. The second-best on his list, Leo shrewdly guessed, should make a good home for the Steins. It did have disadvantages, however. The entrance to the apartment building was a large door at the sidewalk's edge on the rue de Fleurus. That led, and still leads, into a large, paved courtyard. Across the courtyard was the Stein apartment. It was on two levels, ground floor and second story. Furthermore it was a makeshift arrangement in two separate parts. To pass from one to the other, rain or shine, day or night, it was necessary to take a few steps in the courtyard (a covered way was constructed later to connect the two areas). The quarters were cramped and the rent must have been next to nothing. Some American writers whose idea of the proper way of life is a swimming pool and expensive cars would consider this apartment beneath their dignity. But 27 rue de Fleurus became one of the famous literary addresses of this century. From 1903 to 1913 it was the Gertrude Stein-Leo Stein home. Alice B. Toklas moved in with the Steins in 1909 and Leo moved out four years later. From 1913 to 1938 it was the Gertrude Stein-Alice B. Toklas home.

Leo suffered on and off from a desire to paint. This interest receded, fortunately it seems. He turned to theorizing about art, studying it and collecting it. During the summers spent in Fiesole overlooking Florence he concentrated on the treasures of the Renaissance. Yet he did see some Cézanne paintings in a private collection—Cézanne died in 1906. Where could he find more of them in Paris? Bernard Berenson recommended the Ambroise Vollard gallery. It was there that Leo and Gertrude together decided on the *Portrait of Madame Cézanne,* the woman who breathed down Gertrude's neck while she wrote.

They already had bought some other canvases. One was by the nineteenth-century painter Honoré Daumier. Works by Auguste Renoir and Paul Gauguin also hung on the rue de Fleurus walls. These were highly respectable choices. But the Stein taste for collecting sharpened and an irresistible curiosity led them on. Popular favorites did not appeal to them. They would not buy an artist simply because someone else did . . . any more than Gertrude Stein would write what other writers were writing. They made up their own minds. They were absolutely independent.

And they worked at this. They didn't browse, they scrutinized, they inspected. A gallery wasn't merely an agreeable place, it more nearly resembled a laboratory. They looked at a picture in all possible lights. They pored over it, argued about it, fought over it. Pictures were precious to them. One purchase of Leo's incensed Gertrude. When she learned of it at dinner, she threw down her knife and fork in anger. She swore she wouldn't have it around. A wealthy friend was attracted in later years to a Cézanne canvas . . . Cézannes by then commanded a lot of money. This friend went to look at that painting every single morning for an entire month. It could almost be said that by the time of her purchase she knew as much about it as Cézanne. The Steins investigated just as exhaustively. Looking at pictures was fun or they wouldn't have looked. It was also study.

It was not chance or luck but laboriously acquired expertise that led Leo and Gertrude to buy their first truly modern painting. In 1905 they hunted diligently through the Salon d'Automne. This Autumn Salon of paintings was a huge show. Some paintings must have been rejected by the juries but there couldn't have been many. One exhibitor was an unknown by the name of Henri Matisse. One of his submissions was entitled *La Femme au Chapeau* ("Woman with Hat"). A daring slash of green cuts down through the middle of the model's face. It is surmounted by a soaring, monumental, fanciful hat. Some visitors standing in front of the painting burst into mocking laughter. One infuriated viewer tried to scratch off some of the offending paint. Gertrude Stein and Leo drank it all in soberly. At first they did not particularly like the canvas. Yet they couldn't leave it alone . . . or it wouldn't leave them alone. They looked at it again and again.

Gertrude would report that "we" bought it. Leo, contradicting her, would claim that "I" bought it. Whatever the case, it was an all-Stein purchase. They proposed giving a little less than the artist's asking price. The gallery secretary informed the Matisses of the prospective purchase. Henri Matisse was all for accepting the cash actually offered. His canny wife ruled against it. If somebody wanted the painting at all, somebody would pay the full price, she argued. So the Stein-Steins did . . . about one hundred dollars.

It hung in the Stein salon. Stylistically it harmonized more with the Cézanne than with the Daumier or the Gauguin. Now the brother and sister went out and found a painting even closer akin to the Matisse. It was Leo—about this there is no dispute—who first spotted the new man in the tiny shop of Clovis Sagot. Sagot sold paints to painters and sometimes displayed their wares. He was an ex–circus clown. One of his clients was a Spaniard named Pablo Picasso. Picasso had been living in Paris only a few years and was close to starving. His home was a room or two in a tumbledown building way on the other side of the city, high on the steep slope of Montmartre. The building was shaped like one of the laundry barges anchored in the Seine River, roughly like one of our mobile homes. Hence it was called the *Bateau Lavoir*, or Laundry Boat.

Matisse was neat and orderly. His frugal wife operated a small millinery business. It must have been one of her modish hats on display in the Stein purchase. She helped pay the bills while her husband produced paintings that so far hadn't paid any bills at all. Their apartment on the river front overlooked Notre Dame Cathedral. There was a staid, middle-class bourgeois air about them.

Picasso was the complete opposite . . . a hard worker and a dedicated one, too, but carefree, fancy-free, and leading an unconventional life. When the Steins met him, his mistress was the lovely and willowy Fernande Olivier. Their place was anything but neat and orderly. Fernande later visited the studio where he had worked in Barcelona in his native Spain. On its walls the ingenious Picasso had painted pictures of some of the furniture he could not afford to buy. It gave the place the look of a theater, Fernande said. In Paris he was a little better off. Actually having chairs and tables, even though they were broken down, he got along without the make-believe. Whenever he saved a few francs he carried them in a pocket that he fastened with a safety pin.

The art dealer Sagot noted his visitors' interest in a Picasso painting. Would they like to see some other works of Picasso's? Sagot would ask the young artist to bring in a selection. One of them bore the title *Young Girl with Basket of Flowers*. Leo and his sister looked to their heart's content. Sagot, always the businessman, always chewing on a plug of licorice, suggested they might prefer half the painting. He would have Picasso cut off the bottom and leave just the nude bust. After thinking about it the Steins decided they wanted all of her.

Regardless of which one plunged originally into the purchase of moderns, in the end Gertrude Stein remained faithful to them and the more traditional Leo gave them up. In a few years the two would separate. By that time Leo believed he had been all wrong about Picasso, who, in his opinion, had failed as a painter. So when the Stein collection was divided, he took the Renoirs and Matisses. Gertrude, by her emphatic wish, hung onto the Picassos.

These purchases were romantic, memorable and historic events in modern art. In the first decade of this century two unknown painters were hand-picked by two unknown American art lovers. This gave the two artists a leg up on their climb to renown. To a degree it performed a comparable service for the two art lovers. Would someone else have performed this service if the Steins had not? Probably. Yet it *was* the Stein pair that did this. They deserve the credit. Is it not fair also to grant the lion's share of the credit to the sister? She, almost alone as an experimental writer, had the eyes to see what Picasso all alone had the eyes to paint. There was a mysterious affinity. Fate brought them together. But each one had unwittingly studied to prepare himself for this fruitful encounter.

There is another aspect to this conjunction of a quartet

of stars: the two Steins, Picasso and Matisse. Gertrude and her brother were devoted to the new and different. Paris offered countless examples. The city was the seedbed of artists. Hundreds and thousands of men and women were painting there on street corners, in attics, at the Academy of Fine Arts, in schools. Of those thousands we remember today only a few score at the most. The question is, How could Leo and Gertrude have picked the two leading painters of their era out of this vast, faceless, undifferentiated mass? How did they know, seventy years ago, that Picasso and Matisse would become such revered names? Can we go, can you go, to galleries today and select the Picasso and Matisse of the year 2025?

It takes genius to be the Gertrude Stein kind of writer. It also takes genius to be the Gertrude–Leo Stein kind of connoisseur. They had at a rough estimate two chances of winning out of twenty-five thousand. And they won. Easy words for it are "flair" and "knack." We also know the two were steeped in contemporary art. They were enthusiastically receptive to the untried and fresh, they had the open minds advocated by William James. But even all this falls short of explaining their phenomenal foresight. All we can do is salute it and acknowledge that it was unique. It is true, of course, that Picasso helped make Gertrude Stein famous and that Gertrude Stein helped make Picasso famous. But in general the writer made her own way, the artist made his own way.

Now the two set out for a while side by side. Picasso in his mid-twenties had not painted from a model for years. His Rose and Blue periods lay behind him. He was about

Pablo Picasso, *The Reservoir, Horta*. (Private collection, New York)

through with clowns, circus characters and harlequins. He was on the verge of the Cubist creations that would bowl over the art world. Then at Sagot's shop he saw Gertrude Stein. "Who is she?" he asked. He was told she was the sister in the team considering the purchase of a Picasso oil, no less. With only that to go on, he proposed painting her portrait. She liked the idea and said yes.

She enjoyed the calm of posing . . . motionless, silent and relaxed. For four or five months she went to the *Bateau Lavoir* studio day after day. One account of hers reported eighty sittings and another between eighty and ninety. The studio was on the other side of the city. Usually she took what was the contemporary mode of transportation: the horsecar. Sometimes she walked . . . she loved to walk. She was always on the alert for fresh sights and sounds. What she happened to see in a morning or afternoon stroll would be apt to appear in the manuscript on which she labored that same evening.

Picasso sat to do his work in a straight-backed kitchen chair. Gertrude Stein occupied a broken-down armchair. She leaned forward, one hand resting on her knee, the other drooping over the front edge of her lap. A scarf was fastened at her throat with a pin. Sometimes she just sat and looked ahead blankly. At other times Fernande Olivier read in French to her. One day Picasso suddenly declared he could no longer see her face. There and then he painted it out. He and Fernande ran off to Spain for the summer. When he returned he at once painted the face in again without even one more look at his sitter. And it was done.

The face is some Gertrude Stein, some Pablo Picasso and

"... the only reproduction of me which is always I, for me." Pablo Picasso, *Portrait of Gertrude Stein.*

some mask. It tends to abstraction. That is to say, it is part representational and part made up. The eyes are different shapes and sizes. The lids, instead of being curved as in nature, are triangular. The hairline above the brow is drawn arbitrarily. Faces with features related to these would appear in the painting that heralded the birth of Cubism: Picasso's *Les Demoiselles d'Avignon.* The Stein *Portrait* is a key painting of our time. It possesses the double appeal of the pioneering sitter and the pioneering painter. It captures them both in their prime. Stylistic elements show Picasso's gradual movement from one period to another.

The painter gave the portrait to the sitter. In after years he explained that, in view of the prices usual in those days, he did about as well financially in giving it as he would have in selling it. Anyway, the Steins were buying other canvases of his.

Other artists painted Gertrude Stein, sculptors sculptured her and there were innumerable photographs. But the Picasso *Portrait,* she said, was "the only reproduction of me which is always I, for me." She bequeathed it to New York's Metropolitan Museum of Art.

9 *What is known as work is something that I cannot do.*

—EVERYBODY'S AUTOBIOGRAPHY

At the rue de Fleurus paintings climbed right up the walls. When the Steins began their purchases there was room to hang them in a single line at eye level around the studio. Then one had to hang above another, and more even higher. Georges Braque, now a friend now a rival of Picasso, was a particularly welcome visitor. He was so tall he could drive nails in far above where anyone else could reach. Museums have the habit of devoting an entire wall to a single canvas to show it off. At the Steins' a score or more of the most important paintings of the twentieth century were plastered solid all over the walls, frame rubbing against frame.

Inevitably the renown of this collection spread. So did word that author Gertrude Stein in person also was worth seeing. Though some callers came out of sheer curiosity, most of them were serious-minded. They were other art lovers, other collectors, other writers. They were critics, painters, students, scholars. For a while they showed up at all hours. They were so many they impinged on Gertrude Stein's time. So they were concentrated in one night a week, the celebrated Saturday night salon at 27 rue de Fleurus. There were other salons in Paris, one for instance hosted by another American, Natalie Clifford Barney. But few were a match for this one. A guest or two or three might come for dinner. The dining room was little bigger than a postage stamp. The crowd gathered afterward. One of the completely unknown persons to attend would be Alice B. Toklas. She developed into one of the most famous.

Michael Stein settled his father's estate and severed his association with the streetcar business. In 1903 he, his wife, Sarah, and their only child, Allan, moved to Paris to join the brother and sister already there. They took an apartment only a few minutes from the rue de Fleurus. Michael was the only able man of affairs, in the traditional sense, in that clan. Suspecting that his brothers and sisters couldn't earn a living, he set up incomes for them. Gertrude and Leo, properly grateful, were fairly sure he was right about them. It was an odd misjudgment all around. Leo, to be sure, had little money at the time of his death. Michael and Sarah accumulated a modest fortune in Matisse oils. Gertrude, the most imaginative in the whole family, also proved in the long run to be the most "practical." Having her head in the clouds would make her the richest of them all.

To Fernande Olivier, Gertrude and Leo Stein actually

The Steins at Fiesole, 1905. Clockwise: Leo, Michael, Allan, Sarah, and
Gertrude. (The woman with the hat and the girl are unidentified.)

were "rich" Americans. Each one seems, however, to have received a monthly income of slightly under two hundred dollars. Even seventy years ago that provided few luxuries. But it assured a modicum of comfort and it was dependable. It went a long way in the Paris of the first decades of this century. Hélène, the servant of Gertrude Stein and Miss Toklas, could set their table for two dollars a day. That included food for many guests. Matisse, starting out in Paris, managed with a little help from his home on ten dollars a month. So two hundred dollars allowed for some splurging in art purchases.

In 1906 the great earthquake rocked San Francisco. Michael and Sarah returned to the city to see how much damage had been done to their property. They took with them probably the first Matisse paintings to reach their country. It was on this occasion that Miss Toklas met the husband and wife.

Miss Toklas was of Polish-Jewish descent. She had studied to become a concert pianist. Like the Stein children, she had lost her mother. In the 1900's she was marking time, keeping house for her father and brother. Hearing firsthand from the Michael Steins all about Paris, she decided she'd like to go there. A small legacy from her grandfather made the trip possible. In 1907, in the company of a friend, Harriet Levy, she sailed to Europe. There for the first time she made Gertrude Stein's acquaintance. When Leo and his sister moved to Florence for the winter, Harriet Levy and Miss Toklas went, too. Next year, when Harriet Levy returned to the States, Miss Toklas stayed in Paris. In 1909

Alice B. Toklas and Gertrude Stein in Venice, 1908.

she was invited to join the rue de Fleurus *ménage* and make it a threesome.

There is some puzzlement about her original status. Leo remarks that he "had" Alice do some typing for him. Was it her obligation to do this? Or was she merely being obliging? She typed Gertrude Stein's *The Making of Americans*, too. That was a formidable task, and all the more formidable because the typewriter was a cumbersome office model. A bulging tin cover protected it from dust. Was *The Making* again a duty or was Miss Toklas being unofficially helpful? Later Gertrude Stein referred to her as "my secretary." Miss Toklas signed letters in that capacity. Facetious or not, she also identified herself as housekeeper, gardener, needlewoman and "a pretty good vet for dogs."

Gertrude Stein, domestically, was highly impractical. "What is known as work is something that I cannot do," she admitted, or boasted, in *Everybody's Autobiography*. What is known as work was, on the contrary, something that Miss Toklas did admirably. Miss Toklas had been doing just that when she left California. A photograph shows Gertrude Stein standing by a kitchen stove peering down into a bubbling pot. She undoubtedly peered, she undoubtedly never stirred. Miss Toklas did the stirring. Except when father Daniel Stein had fired the cook, Gertrude Stein had nothing to do with kitchens. Once, on the Stein tour of the United States, a news photographer seeking an action shot suggested that she telephone. She replied that she never phoned, Miss Toklas did that for her. The photographer asked her to pack or unpack her suitcase. Again she replied that she never did that either. Miss Toklas did. The photographer finally settled for getting her to drink a glass of water . . . something she did wholly on her own.

Perhaps Miss Toklas' position at the start was workaday and practical. Eventually, of course, it changed. For years she was the most important person in Gertrude Stein's life. Leo, long an essential companion to his sister, found a friend whom he married. He moved out after Miss Toklas moved in.

Michael and his wife, Sarah, became the Matisse enthusiasts. Sarah helped the painter form a class and she enrolled in it. Leo admired Matisse, but more for his attitudes and thoughts than for his painting. Leo had inherited some of his father's dogmatism. He liked to lay down the law. He told Picasso what he should do. He told Matisse what he should not do. Strutting before the paintings in the Stein atelier, he lectured about them. Picasso went to the rue de Fleurus and listened to Leo a while, and then, more enjoyably, he said, looked at Gertrude. She called Leo a village-explainer. That, she added, was "excellent if you were a village, but if you were not, not." In the same chilling terms she dismissed the expatriate poet Ezra Pound.

For more than thirty years Gertrude Stein had idolized her brother. She had accepted him as the elder, the male, the more learned, and she was the docile little sister. Now the tables were turned. Usurping his role, she had blossomed into the important Stein. He acknowledged her possession of a talent and capability denied to him: she could write creatively. Even though he did not like what she did or how she did it, she could do and he could not.

At the same time he was severely critical of Picasso's

Henri Matisse, *Portrait of Michael Stein*. (San Francisco Museum of Art.)

work. About this Leo was consistent. Picasso was breaking away from conventional painting exactly as Gertrude Stein was breaking away from conventional writing. Leo liked the Picasso of the Stein *Portrait*. But Picasso kept changing his style or manner or treatment. The painting he did one day was unlike the painting he would do the next. He was the master of an infinite variety. There was the Picasso of the Blue Period, of the Rose Period, of the Classic Period. He was not one painter, he was ten or twenty. He moved radically away from the representational. What he saw in faces, in landscapes, in still lifes on a table was not good enough for a picture. He rearranged to suit his unique fancy, he distorted. That is, he put together the kind of picture that he liked. He abstracted what seemed to him pictorial in nature and omitted the rest. He liked the shapes and colors, say, of an apple, a pitcher, a woman's cheek. He used them, however, not to make an apple or pitcher or cheek but to make shapes and colors that pleased his exacting eye. All this alienated Leo. Picasso painting and Gertrude Stein writing were lumped together—and in a way they rightly belonged together—by the disgruntled Leo. Then he dismissed them curtly as "godalmighty rubbish." With that, Leo decamped to spend the rest of his life in Italy.

It is hard to determine just how much bitterness developed. Leo had lorded it over Gertrude for years and some resentment on her part was justifiable. She brusquely elbowed him aside and so some resentment on his part, also, was understandable. Outsiders were not helpful. They spread gossip about ill feeling. I think Gertrude Stein merely regarded the association as ended and was willing not to

73

resume it. Before I knew of the quarrel I asked her if she had read a book I said I liked: Leo's *The A-B-C of Aesthetics*. She acted as though she hadn't heard. I asked again and she replied bluntly, in a manner to put me in my place, that she hadn't read it. That put Leo in his place, too. Miss Toklas would not have been so noncommittal. Leo, for his part, may have wanted later to see his sister again. His violent dislike for her writing did not affect his personal attitude, he claimed.

For a while Gertrude Stein and Miss Toklas thought of moving. Instead they had some improvements made at the rue de Fleurus. In place of the original oil lamps the apartment was piped for gas. Next it was wired for electricity. A covered way was built to connect the separate sections of the living quarters. Miss Toklas settled into the relationship as Pussy. Gertrude became Lovey. Years later their friend Carl Van Vechten christened Miss Toklas Mama Woojums, himself Papa Woojums and Gertrude Stein Baby Woojums.

An army of callers invaded this art and literary center. From the United States came, among many others, the Cone sisters of Baltimore. Miss Etta Cone was conscripted, as Miss Toklas had been, to type some Stein manuscripts. Claribel was a doctor, though, like Gertrude Stein and William James, she had never managed to practice. The Cones had a lot of money and spent it generously on paintings. At the start their choices depended considerably on the Steins' advice. They wound up with a Matisse collection second in their country only to the Barnes Foundation's canvases and murals in Merion, Pennsylvania. The Cone collection is now the special treasure of the Baltimore Museum.

The studio at 27 rue de Fleurus. The *Portrait of Madame Cézanne* hangs at Gertrude Stein's right, and Picasso's *The Architect's Table* is on the wall behind her.

Sometimes when Picasso was badly in need of funds Gertrude Stein was unable to help him. She would then steer the Cones up to the *Bateau Lavoir*. They would buy twenty or thirty dollars' worth of sketches and drawings.

Picasso became Gertrude Stein's special care. According to her memoirs she saw a lot of him and Fernande. When Miss Toklas arrived in Paris the artist and his mistress were on the verge of separating. If they did, Fernande would need money. Gertrude Stein rushed Miss Toklas to the rescue. The newcomer would pay Fernande for French lessons.

The hard feelings that persisted between Picasso and Fernande were due, amusingly, to the Katzenjammer Kids. This was a vastly popular comic strip in American newspapers. Gertrude Stein, avant-garde writer, supplied Picasso, avant-garde artist, with these strips that appealed in theory to anybody and everybody except avant-gardists. Picasso loved them and pored over them devotedly. When Fernande left his bed and board, she resented the fact that the cartoons still were sent to him. The one mean, stingy thing about him, she complained, was that he didn't let her enjoy them, too.

10 *I know so well what I mean. They say not but I do.*

—FOUR IN AMERICA

Publishers were indifferent, mocking or rude. One London editor returned a manuscript saying, "I cannot read your M.S. three or four times. Not even one time. Only one look, one look is enough. Hardly one copy would sell here. Hardly one. Hardly one." Other rejections were also couched in this sarcastic vein. However enthusiastic Gertrude Stein's own friends might be, some outsiders were hostile.

Years and years of such negative responses were discouraging. Practical woman that she was, Gertrude Stein decided to try something else. If long works could not sell, perhaps shorter ones would. Magazine publishers might be more receptive. They didn't have so much to lose. Besides, many little magazines in that period were being founded to provide an audience for experimental, noncommercial writing.

One of Gertrude Stein's first ventures was portraits. Paintings fascinated her, we know. They also influenced her in numerous ways. If painters could do pictures of her, she could do pictures of them . . . word pictures. Among her first subjects were, naturally, her first two painter friends, Picasso and Matisse. Their names were the titles of their portraits. These two works, happily, won over a publisher, Alfred Stieglitz, who operated an avant-garde gallery in New York. The gallery was called "291" from its Madison Avenue number. In its way it was as well known as the "27" of the rue de Fleurus. Stieglitz had been an enthusiastic advocate of the Paris modernists. Patrons of his gallery were already familiar with canvases by Picasso and Matisse. His magazine, *Camera Work*, printed Gertrude Stein's two portraits.

They are pen portraits, evocations, re-creations. In theory they are not about Picasso and Matisse, they are substitutes for Picasso and Matisse. Some readers are puzzled by *all* the portraits Gertrude Stein "painted," bar none. Even the most sympathetic readers are puzzled by some of them. They are composed of pickups, they are off the cuff, they are odds and ends. A German painter, Kurt Schwitters, made pictures out of leftovers, chance objects, stray disparate materials. They were impersonal collections. They revealed nothing at all about him except what rubbish heaps he had visited. The Stein portraits, less impersonal, are, however, just as random. It would help in understanding them if we had been with her in the hours or days before they were created. Then we would know what she had seen or heard or what she had turned over in her mind. The portraits are not automatic writing. They are accurate, detailed representations of her subject and the envelope around it. Out of haphazard sounds and sights and encounters she put together a whole.

At a later date she did a second Picasso portrait: "If I Told Him: A Completed Portrait of Picasso." It begins:

> If I told him would he like it. Would
> he like it if I told him.
> Would he like it would Napoleon would
> Napoleon would would he like it.

Where does Napoleon come from? Gertrude Stein used to see Picasso, a diminutive figure, in the company of a quartet of stalwarts: André Derain, André Salmon, Georges Braque and Guillaume Apollinaire. They were his painter and writer friends. She compared him to the diminutive Napoleon escorted by four oversize grenadiers. Hence we get the reference in the portrait. A key helps. Even without it the rhythm and flow of the words catch your attention. There are songs without words. This is words without song. The effect is the same. There is a perverse pleasure in not knowing at first glance what you are reading. Mumbo jumbo is a kind of fun.

The most famous of these creations is *The Portrait of Mabel Dodge at the Villa Curonia*. It was written in 1912. Mabel Dodge was a wealthy American married to an American architect, Edwin Dodge. They lived outside Florence in a villa he had remodeled. She provided hospitable entertainment for celebrities and near-celebrities. Among her visitors were Gertrude and Leo Stein and Miss Toklas. The portrait begins, "The days are wonderful and the nights are wonderful and the life is pleasant." This obviously describes the good time the author is enjoying. The portrait ends, "There is not all of any visit." This is to say that she can't thank Mabel Dodge enough; she has written her bread-and-butter letter on the spot. The thirty-five hundred words contain references to furniture, garden, bedding, packing, running water, walks, floors, food and so on. The materials, that is, are picked right out of the days and nights, the Dodges, the servants, the villa, the grounds, the entire scene and setting. Such things aren't observed in a connected fashion. They just appeared to Gertrude Stein one after another in the course of the visit. So, in the same way, they appear one after another in the portrait. The dramatic person of Mabel Dodge ties them all together. They furnish an air, an ambiance. They are conjured up. A medium might call them ectoplasm.

Some readers can make neither head nor tail of this. They don't mind saying so, either. Mabel Dodge herself was delighted. Wasn't it as important to be word-painted by Gertrude Stein as to be painted in oils by Picasso or Matisse? She had in fact been portrayed beautifully by the artist Jacques Émile Blanche. Gertrude Stein's portrait of her was brand-new, revolutionary. But she, too, confessed to some puzzlement. Certain passages baffled her. She was an introspective woman and some aspects of her actual physical self and psyche baffled her, too. Obviously the astute Gertrude Stein had detected certain secret characteristics that had eluded her hostess. Given time and patience the veil would be lifted. She, too, might learn what hitherto had been hidden. People who sit for their portraits are very easily offended. They are not flattered enough, an impartial outsider is apt to believe. They themselves complain that their unique qualities have been slighted or ignored. But here was an eminently satisfied sitter.

Mrs. Dodge was no one to hide her light—if light it was —under a bushel. She sent the portrait to a printer. Another Villa Curonia guest, Constance Fletcher, an American writer, proofread it. It must be remembered that this was a substantial service. Words arranged in the normal sequence can be checked with comparative ease. With Gertrude Stein's prose, this could be extraordinarily difficult. The author herself and Miss Toklas nearly wore out their eyes proofreading *The Making of Americans*.

Several hundred copies of *The Portrait of Mabel Dodge* were bound in fancy Florentine paper. Packing them up, Mrs. Dodge carted them off with her to New York. She arrived just in time for the famous 1913 Armory Show. This was a revolutionary event on the American art calendar. At long last American audiences had a good overall look at the true moderns, the Paris moderns in particular. In Chicago and Boston, to which the exhibit also traveled, some viewers admired, some laughed, some were outraged. One painting was burned in effigy. But New Yorkers were more sophisticated. If they didn't accept it all, they put up with it. There were many Cubist paintings, and controversial works like Marcel Duchamp's *Nude Descending a Staircase*. Among the painters exhibited were Braque, Cézanne, Daumier, Derain, Gauguin, Vasili Kandinski, Fernand Léger, Matisse, Alfred Maurer, Edvard Munch, Jules Pascin, Francis Picabia, Picasso, Odilon Redon, Georges

Rouault, Georges Seurat, Henri de Toulouse-Lautrec. Half a dozen of them came right out of the Gertrude Stein circle. Mabel Dodge collected some of the proposed exhibits from the New York owners. Whenever she rang a doorbell and picked up a painting, she left a copy of *The Portrait of Mabel Dodge at the Villa Curonia*. That spread Gertrude Stein's name around and did no harm to Mabel Dodge's, either. It was this work that first attracted the interest of Carl Van Vechten, who later became Gertrude Stein's close friend. About this time, too, Henry McBride of the New York *Sun*, most sympathetic of the columnists, entered the lists in Gertrude Stein's behalf.

The word *synaesthesia* denotes the transfer of impressions from one sense to another. You see a bright red, the effect you feel is that of a loud bang. Gertrude Stein's technique in these portraits was synaesthetic. It was a turnabout. She was doing for Picasso, say, in pen and ink what he had done for her in color. It was tit for tat, word for oil. The color of the character was registered in the black and white of the printed page.

There is some appearance of incongruity in the materials of the portraits. This is also true of the artists' paintings. At first glance they do not always, as we say, jell. You are supposed to look again and again, like the Stein friend contemplating the purchase of a Cézanne. It is only fair to give the pen portraits as well as the oil paintings a chance. As Gertrude Stein had been obliged to keep her mind open, the reader must keep his open, too. If you do not get a meaning out of a picture, you may still get a feeling. "Why does a picture have to have a meaning?" the exasperated Picasso asked in response to questions about his sometimes enigmatic works. This query was commonly inspired by oils in the Armory Show. There was, for instance, the Duchamp *Nude Descending a Staircase*. We have noted the writer . . . say Stein . . . following the trail of the painter . . . say Picasso. Is not Duchamp in the repetitions or reiterations of his jittery figure following the writer's trail? Experiment and adventure were in the air. Anyone living in those exciting and stirring days was exposed to exciting and stirring ideas.

The most impressive odds-and-ends composition from the Stein palette, or writing table, is called *Tender Buttons*. The subtitle indicates its division into three sections: *Objects Food Rooms*. Even some friendly critics balk at this book. Who ever heard of tender buttons? they ask in annoyance. The answer is that nobody had, so it was high time to spread the news around.

The book marks a change . . . I would say advance . . . in the Gertrude Stein style. Painters have "periods": early, middle, late, rose, blue, harlequin and so on. Writers can have periods, too. Here was the new Stein period. In essence it was Cubist. She and Miss Toklas had spent the summer of 1912 in Spain. Gertrude Stein traipsed around in brown corduroys, with a small crocheted cap. Miss Toklas was in funereal black coat and gloves. Mooning about in the Alhambra, the ancient Moorish capital in Granada, Gertrude Stein had experienced some sort of change. People had mattered to her before. Now things began to matter. Her interest was shifting from people to people's surroundings. She was interested in the inanimate, with the aim of rendering

Marcel Duchamp, *Nude Descending a Staircase*. (Philadelphia
Museum of Art: The Louise and Walter Arensberg Collection.)

it animate. Thus she took a bold step toward the "land-scapes" that would eventually turn into "plays."

Tender Buttons consists of perfect pen-and-ink still lifes. Picasso had begun to feel his way into Cubism some years before. As Gertrude Stein used "objects food rooms," Picasso used faces, landscapes, bodies, furniture. His paintings are composed of planes in various geometric shapes. He made them out of these shapes rather than out of the actual surfaces from which he arbitrarily lifted them. He worked, that is, from squares, circles, triangles, cubes . . . Cubism. Gertrude Stein did the same with the materials of her choice. She picked them up, toyed with them, shuffled them around.

And she hit on the matchless title. One critic has suggested that "tender buttons" are simply means of joining things together. Someone else regards them as the nipples of breasts. In my opinion tender buttons are just tender buttons, tender comma buttons, no more. They are incongruous, impossible, disparate parts of different things run graphically together. They are no stranger, no harder to accept, no more in need of exegesis than phrases from another Stein book, *The Gertrude Stein First Reader and Three Plays*. There we have "careless butter," "anxious milk," "angry spinach" and "morose cabbage." If there is spice in the "food" section of *Tender Buttons*, there is just as much in "objects" and "rooms." Only an endlessly inventive mind could run these words together. I find them fun; but more than that, too.

Here is language used in such a way as to acquire a fresh and more solemn value. The one thing you cannot do with

Pablo Picasso, *The Architect's Table*. Among the objects on the table the artist painted the calling card of Miss Gertrude Stein. (Collection, The Museum of Modern Art, New York.)

Gertrude Stein is read fast. Courses that teach you to absorb a page at a glance don't help at all with *Tender Buttons.* That is one of this author's virtues. The writing is not only an entertainment, it is also a discipline. The author obliges the eye and, along with it, the mind to halt at every cluster of letters. "Stop look and listen," she orders us. We are getting used to food processed and packaged. She gives it to us raw. This is a kind of do-it-yourself writing and reading. You go through her pages as a child goes through his first reader. You put your finger under one word after another. This sort of slow motion enables you to relish all the book's exotic flavor.

Carl Van Vechten was instrumental in getting *Tender Buttons* into print. A friend of his, Donald Evans, had founded an experimental publishing house, Claire-Marie— in New York, unexpectedly, not Paris. Claire-Marie brought out this short book in 1914. You can read it all at one sitting. It is better, though, to sample it as you might a collection of aphorisms. A few quotations show its nature. The flavor is rather literary than gastronomic, though the first phrases reprinted here come from the section called "food":

CHICKEN

Alas a dirty word, alas a dirty third alas a dirty third, alas a dirty bird.

And then still more:

A cup is neglected by being all in size. It is a handle and meadows and sugar any sugar . . .
Why is a cup a stir and a behave. Why is it so seen.

A cup is readily shaded, it has in between no sense that is to say music, memory, musical memory.
Peanuts blame, a half sand is holey and nearly.

Gertrude Stein's interest in food in these pages is the exact opposite of Miss Toklas'. After Gertrude Stein's death her companion wrote two cookbooks. A cup was no behave and a chicken was no dirty third to Miss Toklas. She wrote from the point of view of the kitchen. Gertrude Stein wrote from the point of view not even of the dining room but of the study. Miss Toklas was being practical, Gertrude Stein was being Cubist not to say ecstatic. Henri Matisse was asked about a tomato. Was the tomato he saw when he ate it the same as the one he saw when he painted it? No, not at all, he said. There was the same Stein-Toklas art-food difference. The food Miss Toklas cooked . . . and cooked marvelously . . . was worlds away from the food in *Tender Buttons*.

Some subtitles are intriguing: "A Mounted Umbrella," "A Piece of Coffee," "A Carafe, That is a Blind Glass," "A Method of a Cloak," "A Little Called Pauline," "It Was Black, Black Took." Under "objects" we find these uncookbook-like statements:

> Lax, to have corners, to be lighter than some weight, to indicate a wedding journey, to last brown and not curious, to be wealthy, cigarettes are established by length and by doubling.
> The sudden spoon is the wound in the decision.
> A letter was nicely sent.
> Please a round it is ticket.

Couldn't some of this, you wonder, be turned back into a Cubist painting? Painter and writer alike use parts and pieces. In essence they are interchangeable. What goes on paper goes as well on canvas. Once in a while Gertrude Stein puns. Once in a while she slips into an obvious rhyme like word, bird and third. These are not her most impressive or successful creations. Once in a while, too, the repetition is so startling, so dramatic, so odd, that it earns its own inviolable niche in our literature. Two years before *Tender Buttons* she wrote "Sacred Emily." It was not a particularly inspired work, or so she herself concluded. Quite a few of the short pieces of these years are trial runs rather than meaningful poems or portraits. "Sacred Emily," we are told, was abandoned. The indifferent author brushed it aside. Miss Toklas supposedly rescued it and so saved what is perhaps the most quoted of all Steiniana: "Rose is a rose is a rose is a rose."

On other occasions Gertrude Stein would vary this. Sometimes there are only three roses. Sometimes the succession of words begins with the indefinite article *a*: "a rose" instead of "rose." Some quizzical students asked her what in the world she meant by these repetitions. She replied that of course she knew people didn't say "is a . . . is a . . . is a." It was a sly defense. Nobody was objecting to "is a . . . is a . . . is a" but to "rose . . . rose . . . rose . . . rose." Elsewhere she justified it on theoretical grounds. This sentence epitomized what she was trying to do with language, she claimed. Words have lost much of their original fire and sparkle. We take them for granted. Words, like print on the pages of musty books, have faded. Used over and over for centuries, they are blurred, they are limp, the edges are worn. Her phrase, she said, turned the rose red again for the first time since Shakespeare. It was red for the first time, that is, since English was in its pristine vigor and force. One critic praising the phrase commented that the rose had for the first time again become yellow. Whatever the color, the point is well taken. "Rose" brightened up with new life. Its primeval freshness was restored. You could really smell it.

Run across the word in a sentence and you slide quickly over it. That is, you used to. Gertrude Stein will never let you do that again. Her phrase is simple but it is packed with intimations. At first you snorted, or laughed, or mocked. But you can't keep it up. This rose is a rose for real for real.

The words are arranged to run around a circle. They were embroidered in the corner of the Stein linen. They were engraved on a set of china. They were used as a letterhead. They have fixed themselves immovably in our minds.

11 *There is that something about a war.*

In 1913 Gertrude Stein and Miss Toklas went on a scouting trip to England. Could they perhaps interest a London editor? Gertrude Stein interviewed publisher John Lane but could not pin him down to a contract.

That wonder of wonders did happen, however, the following year. Lane had visited Gertrude Stein in Paris and decided to risk bringing out something of hers. His choice was not venturesome. It was a book already privately printed: *Three Lives.* Did she have something else? She suggested *The Making of Americans,* but that, he feared, was too long. Then she proposed a group of portraits. The negotiations had reached this stage when in the summer the two women crossed the Channel again. They had planned a brief stay. They had not planned on the outbreak of a world war.

Now Miss Toklas met her third genius. In a Gertrude Stein book we shall read about later, Miss Toklas says, "Only three times in my life have I met a genius and each time a bell within me rang." The first bell was for Gertrude Stein. The second bell was for Pablo Picasso. It might have rung for Bertrand Russell, Charlie Chaplin, Sherwood Anderson, Ernest Hemingway, Juan Gris, James Joyce, Henri Matisse and many others. But no. The bell within rang the third and last time when she made the acquaintance of Alfred North Whitehead. He was the philosopher and mathematician who had collaborated with Bertrand Russell on *Principia Mathematica*. For this pioneering work, Gertrude Stein said, Whitehead modestly gave Russell most of the credit.

Dr. and Mrs. Whitehead invited Gertrude Stein and Miss Toklas to stay in Lockridge, their home not far outside London. The Whiteheads were meeting a genius, too . . . not that they kept count . . . and a most congenial one. Gertrude Stein was a marvelously likable person. She loved to talk and she also loved to listen. She listened carefully, too; that is the highest compliment one can pay a speaker. But then she did not neglect to put in her oar. She spoke slowly. Her voice was resonant. The one characteristic everyone remarked about was her hypnotic laugh. It was a great, deep, booming boom. Broad mouth wide open, head tilted back, brown eyes a-glitter, the laugh burst out thunderous and loud. You laughed with this laugh. You couldn't help yourself.

The contract for *Three Lives* was signed with John Lane. Now, for the first time, Gertrude Stein had done business with a highly reputable commercial firm. She and Miss Toklas now went shopping. When Leo had left their home in Paris, they had for a while thought of moving. Now that they were staying in the rue de Fleurus they needed more furniture. They bought some to take back.

All of a sudden they discovered that they couldn't get back themselves. Almost overnight England and France went to war with Germany. The Austrian archduke Francis Ferdinand and his wife had been assassinated in Sarajevo, Serbia, in June. When Gertrude Stein and Miss Toklas sailed for England in July, there was little indication of the catastrophe already brewing. But ominous moments of deathly quiet alternated with ominous diplomatic interchanges. In the very first days of August all Europe found itself in arms. The German invasion of Belgium caught everyone by surprise. It especially threw off balance the French generals and their luckless infantry. Powerful German drives west and south swept everything before them. Resistance collapsed. Paris was threatened. It seemed that the city might once again be occupied by German forces, as it had been in the Franco-Prussian War of 1870–71.

Gertrude Stein and Miss Toklas had settled temporarily with the Whiteheads. There were worthwhile distractions and the two women tried hard to enjoy themselves. But they couldn't. All their worldly goods plus some unworldly things like Picasso paintings were in their rue de Fleurus apartment. The lives of Frenchmen and women of their acquaintance were in danger. A dear American friend in a cottage on the Marne River was threatened by the enemy advance.

Then General Joseph Simon Gallieni, with General Joseph "Papa" Joffre in overall command, conscripted the famous taxicab army in Paris. Thanks to the reinforcements rushed into the front line by streams of autos, the Germans were stopped at the last minute. Though France suffered several more years of torment, Paris was saved. Miss Toklas hurried to tell Gertrude Stein the news. Gertrude Stein didn't believe it. But it was true. And they wept.

For the moment Paris remained out of bounds for maiden ladies stranded in London. The distance was long and the Channel crossing was hazardous. Mrs. Whitehead, however, knew important people, among them the famed Earl Kitchener of Khartoum, statesman and warlord. Through her intercession his office provided travel permits for Gertrude Stein and Miss Toklas. Mrs. Whitehead also arranged to make the trip. Her son was stationed at the front. He needed his overcoat. She took it to him. It was that folksy kind of war in the first months, though casualties mounted eventually to appalling totals.

Nothing had gone wrong in the two Americans' absence. Their things were unmolested. But they were now to live in a wartime capital city. If you never have, you can't imagine what it's like. Lights must not shine through windows at night. The streets are black. Food, fuel and clothing are rationed. Nobody feels sociable. Anyway, many of the people you are normally sociable with have left. During World War I many Americans living in Paris went back to America. Some settled in neutral Spain or Switzerland. Some were burdened with wartime duties, some were in uniform. For a time Gertrude Stein and Miss Toklas resigned themselves to making the best of about the worst of possible situations. Money was scarce. Miss Toklas received funds from her father. Gertrude Stein sold a painting. Even when they had money, most luxuries and some necessities were no longer on sale.

In World War II capital cities would be raided by bombing planes. During its last months Nazi buzz bombs would zero in on London. Toward the end of World War I the Germans (called "Boches" in those years) prepared Big Bertha. This giant cannon lobbed shells into Paris from far behind German lines. But at the start of the first war, the main threat to Paris seemed to be from Zeppelin airship raids. Faced with that grim prospect Gertrude Stein and Miss Toklas sensibly decided to clear out. They went first to Spain and then settled on the Mediterranean island of Mallorca. There they managed . . . but no more than managed. Germans were there, too. Some had gladly fled their warring fatherland. Others were frank sympathizers with Kaiser Wilhelm and his military chiefs. One of them showed defiantly how she felt. At every report of a German victory she ran up the German flag. Gertrude Stein reciprocated. Not many Allied victories were chalked up in those dismal months. But at every one the French Tricolor waved defiantly outside the home of the two Americans.

The Zeppelin-raid scare subsided. Eventually Gertrude Stein and Miss Toklas returned to the rue de Fleurus. Once more they had been lucky. Their belongings had not been disturbed. They resumed their humdrum daily life . . . no real hardships, no real comforts, no real pleasures.

Picasso, a citizen of neutral Spain, was not personally involved in France's struggle. He was left free to paint as Gertrude Stein was left free to write. Once, walking with his American friend along the boulevard Raspail, he saw a French army truck. Its sides were daubed with great colored geometrical shapes. Picasso brightened up. "We did that," he boasted, and he was right. It was Cubism applied as camouflage. An incidental effect of a Cubist picture is to distort a person or object almost to the point of unrecognizability. In the same way a Cubist design distorts a vehicle. It disguises the true shape and outline so that they are hard to define.

Another walk had important consequences. Gertrude Stein and Miss Toklas saw an auto bearing the sign, "American Fund for French Wounded." A uniformed woman driver sat at the wheel. What, they wondered, was that about? Even before the United States had declared war on Germany, American sympathy had been largely with the French. Now some American women volunteers, headed by Mrs. Isabel Lathrop, had organized to distribute supplies to various hospitals.

This, Gertrude Stein decided, was what she very much wanted to do. She would drive, Miss Toklas would distribute. Mrs. Lathrop welcomed the new recruits. All Gertrude Stein needed, she was told, was a car. Lacking the money to buy one, she appealed to relatives in the States. They promptly had a car shipped. As it was the gift of an Aunt Pauline, it was nicknamed Auntie. Years later an uncomplimentary reference to its penchant for balking proved unhappily offensive to the generous donor. The car was a

Ford. It was fitted with a truck body. I remember it very well because I enjoyed a lot of wonderful rides in it.

But Gertrude Stein needed something else that Mrs. Lathrop had failed to mention. She needed to learn to drive. During the Mallorcan sojourn she had met another expatriate American, William Cook. He was now in Paris to learn to paint. Unfortunately he was penniless . . . though a sizable inheritance after the war was to put him on Easy Street in a house built by the modernist Le Corbusier. To earn a living in those early years he resorted to a variety of odd jobs. At this time he was driving a Paris taxicab. It was of the same vintage as the cabs in which Joffre and Gallieni had sped reserve troops to the front in the fall of 1914. It was a poky, high-wheeled, bumbling old Renault. Cook undertook the formidable task of teaching Gertrude Stein to drive.

He was an excellent teacher. She was not an apt pupil. She learned to start the car. In those days that included adjusting the spark, priming the motor, and cranking. She could drive forward with passable competence. But for a time she was unable to go backward at all. Even after years of experience she remained leery of the process of backing. So perhaps Cook didn't really teach her. He only tried. It was one of the things she never really dependably learned. But it is fair to add that she drove better than she cooked, housekept or packed.

To the best of my knowledge she never had an accident. To be sure, a laconic Chicago policeman years later warned her after she made an illegal U-turn, "Well go on, but you will most likely get killed before you leave town." She didn't, but there were near-misses. Once my wife and I drove with her and Miss Toklas to Aix-les-Bains. We rounded a curve at the foot of a long hill. Our intrepid driver not only rounded the curve but also passed a slower car holding us up. That brought us, bang! in front of a car speeding down at us. The brakes slammed on. It threw us forward so we nearly bloodied our noses. The enemy driver leaned out and screamed some French that I would blush to think Gertrude Stein could understand. But it escaped being an accident.

Gertrude Stein very much liked to have her own way. For years people made fun of her writing. For years they refused to publish it. Yet she forged ahead doggedly on the path she had set for herself. She did not let herself be sidetracked. She did not let anyone interfere. She ignored all literary "No passing" signs. For her with pen in hand there were no speed limits. The final results proved everyone else had been wrong and she had been right. She was inclined to regard driving in the same light as writing. It was her car. It was her road. Who would have the nerve to get in the way of Gertrude Stein? On her own for the first time in Paris, the worst she did was to stall. She might have stalled on a quiet street where no one would notice. Instead she picked a boulevard and the middle of streetcar tracks. She tied up traffic and passersby rallied to push her out of the way. But she made it.

At last she and Miss Toklas started on their first assignment to help the French wounded . . . well away from Paris traffic. They were stationed in the old Mediterranean walled town of Perpignan. They occupied quarters in a hotel. It was the depot for their supplies. They delivered medicines, bandages and all sorts of surgical devices to hospitals in that area.

Later they were transferred to Nîmes. One of France's oldest cities, it is wonderfully well stocked with Roman ruins. They are not really in ruins, either. There is an arena in a much better state of preservation than Rome's Colosseum. It is even used nowadays for public spectacles. On a height overlooking the city is the Tour Magne, a tower so old that no one remembers its original purpose. From its summit on a clear day you can see the Mediterranean twenty-five miles away. The city has Roman fountains and baths. Perhaps the prize is the Maison Carrée, once a temple and now a museum. It is small but infinitely more impressive than Paris' great Madeleine Church, which was modeled on it.

"Auntie" was far from streamlined. Its antique headlights threw only feeble beams. They told someone else you were coming. They didn't clearly tell you where you were going. The straight up-and-down windshield was designed in two separate horizontal sections. The upper half wound up to let in a breeze on the driver. A canvas top on a rickety frame swung down over the seat. That helped keep off some rain. The sides had no curtains and were open to the elements. The tires were not much bigger than bicycle tires. The fenders resembled diminutive wings. They sat well above the wheels, which had wooden spokes. Of course there was a crank. There were outside running boards which have not been used on cars for so many years that young

Gertrude Stein and Alice B. Toklas with "Auntie," 1917.

people may not know what they were. The whole machine was spindly like an old-time buggy. Sometimes you wished you had the horse with it. But it always got there, though it wasn't built for speed.

The United States had only recently entered the war. I had been serving with the French army and I was due for a furlough. I wanted to take it as far from the front as possible. I also wanted to see Roman ruins because I had been studying Latin. So I went to Nîmes and got a room in the

100

Hotel Luxembourg. Gertrude Stein and Miss Toklas were staying there. That was where I met them.

They were an odd-looking pair. They were not the answer to a soldier boy's dreams about the girls of Paris. Miss Toklas was short, small and spry. She had a faint trace of a mustache. She was fond of jewelry, none of it expensive, all of it exotic. She and her companion were both dressed in heavy-duty corduroy of a mannish, army-uniform cut, belted and with capacious pockets. The chilly weather of late fall required warm clothing even close to the Mediterranean. Sometimes the headgear the two wore resembled a helmet. Sometimes it was a regular felt hat with a brim. Or it might be toque-shaped. Both women wore sandals. Gertrude Stein was very overweight. But instead of being ungainly, she was statuesque. She moved as though she were on rollers. There was no appearance of effort. Her upper body did not sway, it sort of floated. She took one step to her friend's two. They were a ponderous man-of-war and a speedy destroyer running circles around it.

I came along, luckily, when American soldiers were still a novelty. The two expatriates had seen some of us but not many. I was the only one then in Nîmes. They introduced themselves. I looked so young they called me Kiddie, and later my wife became Mrs. Kiddie. They invited the Kiddie to tea. A table loaded with sweets was set up in the lobby. There were plates with mounds and heaps of frosted cakes. To a soldier who for months had hardly even seen a piece of candy, this was the treat of a lifetime. He dug in.

The hostesses were infinitely rarer than their bounteous fare. They were entitled to a vacation, they said. Would the

101

Kiddie like to drive around the countryside with them? Day after day we went out. The only rule was, get back before nightfall. Miss Stein, said Miss Toklas, did not like to drive after dark. One reason was the feeble headlights. We were late only once. Then the Kiddie shinnied up a pole at an intersection to see which arrow-shaped sign pointed back to Nîmes. Gertrude Stein occupied the driver's half of the seat and, due to the width of her beam, half of the other half. Miss Toklas fitted neatly into the remaining space. The Kiddie sat on the floor with his feet on the running board. Once in a while he had to change a tire. Always he was the one to crank the motor.

He had the vacation to end all vacations. The area around Nîmes is one solid museum stretching for miles; arenas, theaters, churches, aqueducts, Caesarean battlefields. There are Roman, Romanesque, Gothic and Renaissance works not to mention modern . . . the artists Paul Gauguin and Vincent van Gogh lived a while in Arles, and Cézanne was born in Aix-en-Provence. Arles also has a Roman arena and an awesome Roman burial ground. Avignon has the Palace of the Popes and the bridge famed in the folksong, "Sur le pont d'Avignon," where the boys and girls used to dance. Orange can boast of a magnificent ancient theater with tiers of seats cut into the rock of the hillside. From the walled city of Aigues-Mortes King Louis IX, Saint Louis, set out on a crusade. Les Baux is a fabulously picturesque aerie set atop a peaked Alpine foothill. Not far off, in Uzès, the dramatist Jean Baptiste Racine used a pavilion for his study. In the same direction is the superb Pont du Gard, a three-tiered aqueduct that nineteen hundred years ago began to supply Nîmes with water.

The hostess-guides knew all these places, talked about them, pointed out special features. The Kiddie was a completely unknown buck private. They could not have done more for him if he had been the General of the Army, William James, Pablo Picasso or John Lane.

They asked lots of questions. This was a Gertrude Stein technique for building up and filling out her files on the whole human race. Where did the Kiddie come from, who was his father, what did he study at Amherst, how did he happen to come to Nîmes, what would he do after the war, what did he think of President Woodrow Wilson? They were not nosy. They were, on the contrary, friendly. They made him believe Gertrude Stein was interested not only in the human race but also in him.

What did he know about them? Nothing. He had never heard their names. He probably had not heard of the Armory Show. Certainly Picasso and Matisse were as much blanks to him as Stein. All he was told was this brief remark by Miss Toklas: "Miss Stein writes."

These two weeks of sightseeing, more important to him than he can say, counted for little in Gertrude Stein's long life. But they deserve these paragraphs because they show a Stein totally unlike the one that hostile critics have described. Her egotism has been ridiculed. To be sure, she brought the mockers and the doubters down on her own head. "Think of the Bible and Homer think of Shakespeare and think of me" . . . that grouping was an invitation to trouble. "A woman in this epoch does the important literary thinking," she would claim unabashedly. She rarely refrained from figuratively tapping her chest and intoning, "Genius!" But she did refrain during those two weeks.

There was not a single hint of this attitude. She never suggested she was anybody but the (incompetent) driver of a rattling Ford truck with a very hard floor for a seat. She did happen to mention that she lived in Paris. All she did was show the Kiddie the sights, take him to dinner, and be his mentor, guide and chauffeur. And all the time she sort of stood back and took a real delight in the real delight he took in sightseeing.

At the war's end the two women were transferred to northeastern France. At long last they again returned to their abandoned Paris home. Once more their luck had held: no one had touched a thing. They were in the French capital when victory was celebrated. Mrs. Whitehead came over from London for the event. She occupied an apartment overlooking the Champs Élysées. Gertrude Stein and Miss Toklas joined her there for a clear view of the great procession. There were massed flags, trucks and tanks camouflaged with Cubist designs, smart-stepping soldiers, cavalry detachments, colorful uniforms, bands, and dignitaries led by Generals Pétain and Joffre and their American and British peers.

12　*It is always a pleasure to be partial.*

The manuscripts piled up and up in a great wooden chest at the rue de Fleurus. For most of them there was still no publisher. John Lane had brought out two editions of *Three Lives,* one in 1915 and one in 1920. They were based physically and editorially on the original New York edition and they did not even then make a great stir . . . that would come only later. Yet Gertrude Stein's reputation kept growing. The less she was read, the more famous she became. Thanks to the grapevine she amassed an enviable following. There had been the legend of the little boy and girl and their impossible trek in California. Now there developed a legend about an author. This one had substance.

Friends, admirers and followers multiplied. Her three probably best known compatriots were Sherwood Anderson, F. Scott Fitzgerald and Ernest Hemingway. The paths

105

of their lives as novelists crossed in the United States. They crossed also at the rue de Fleurus. They all expressed a debt of some kind to Gertrude Stein. They learned from what she wrote and what she said. They also learned from what she was . . . monumental, confident, dogmatic even, and committed body and soul to her craft and theirs.

Anderson was the closest, dearest and most dependable of the trio. He was also the oldest. Even Miss Toklas, whose likes and dislikes were eccentric, remained fond of Anderson. Gertrude Stein liked Fitzgerald's *This Side of Paradise* and *The Great Gatsby*. She saw in him, she said, the William Makepeace Thackeray of the Age of the Flapper. On her visit to America in 1934–35 she enjoyed two happy reunions. One was with Anderson. The other was with Fitzgerald and his wife, Zelda. Those were their last meetings. But she did not see Hemingway. By that time something between them had soured.

The association with Hemingway was variously affectionate, admiring, cool, indifferent and bitter. At their first meeting he was a newspaperman with an overpowering urge to write. Gertrude Stein thought he was handsome and she liked him a lot. They went on long walks together, they talked endlessly. Could he cut loose from the job at which he earned a living, he asked, and write a novel? She advised him to take a chance and he did. He had to scrimp. He had a wife and a baby boy. Gertrude Stein and Miss Toklas were the godmothers, as they were also the godmothers of Picasso's son.

Hemingway pulled out all the stops in praise of Gertrude Stein and her work. There was nobody like her, he said

Picasso and his son Claude at Bilignin.

more than once. He confessed in a letter to her that writing had not been easy before he met her: "I certainly was bad, gosh, I'm awfully bad now, but it's a different kind of bad." It was not only talk on his part. He tried hard to find a publisher for *The Making of Americans*. Unable to persuade a New York house to shoulder this formidable task, he turned to a new magazine. Ford Madox Ford was about to edit *The Transatlantic Review*. Hemingway was associated with the venture in a subordinate role. Thanks to his persuasiveness Ford undertook to serialize the almost endless novel. But there proved to be no extra copy. Hemingway himself typed one for the printer. As Miss Toklas, speaking for Gertrude Stein in *The Autobiography of Alice B. Toklas*, would say of Hemingway, "He wrote to Gertrude Stein saying that it was she who had done the work in writing The Making of Americans and he and all his had but to devote their lives to seeing that it was published." He also went around planting copies in Paris bookstores when the book was printed by a mutual friend, Robert McAlmon, in Contact Editions.

A lot of Hemingway prose—short, clipped sentences, repetitions, colloquialisms—looks and reads like a lot of Gertrude Stein prose. Some pages in *Three Lives*, published in 1909, could have been written by Hemingway. Some pages in *The Sun Also Rises*, published in 1926, and *A Farewell to Arms*, published in 1929, have an indubitable Gertrude Stein flavor.

But Hemingway was endowed with a sense of drama lacking in Gertrude Stein. That indirectly led to a parting of the ways. He was commercially successful almost from the start. She had a long wait and even so she never came anywhere near catching up with him in public favor. She resented that a little. Why did he sell so well, she once asked me, and she sell so poorly? She thought he was unwisely, perhaps unhealthily, intent on physical prowess. What mattered to him was hair on the chest. His personal failings, which to be sure contributed to his finest writing, were nonetheless failings. She poked mild fun at him in a game played with the poodle Basket. She snapped a man-sized handkerchief up and down before Basket's nose. "Play Hemingway!" she ordered. "Be fierce!" The dog would jump and bark. It was the bull being taunted by the toreador. Hemingway, the bullfight fan, was being mocked . . . harmles ˙ but mocked . . . by his mentor.

A few slighting references to her are scattered throug̣ his work. They seem to me no more vindictive than the aꞇ she put on with Basket. To be sure, she hated rivalry. Aꞇ first she had said she was "slowly . . . knowing that I was a genius." Later she could say frankly, even aggressively, as if to dare anyone to deny it, "I have been the creative literary mind of the century." Anyone running her a close second upset her. It was particularly unpleasant to be outdistanced by a novelist who once had been a nobody.

After she died Hemingway wrote that he certainly hated for Gertrude to be dead. He remembered that he had loved her. He remembered gratefully, too, that he had learned from her what he called "prose rhythms." After Hemingway's death a collection of his essays called A Moveable Feast was published. Some of them contained mean and scurrilous comments about Gertrude Stein. He did write them. Yet it is only fair to him to remember that he himself in his lifetime refrained from publishing them. That was the way he had felt when he wrote. But he never reached the point of saying some of these objectionable things openly. Some incidents in his posthumous work reflected harshly on Fitzgerald and Anderson as well as on Gertrude Stein. At any rate it was Hemingway who quarreled with the three. Gertrude Stein got along with the two others in a friendly way. Should not Hemingway, then, instead of Gertrude Stein be blamed for the disagreements? Miss Toklas evened the score in the end. Asked for her opinion of him, she retorted that it was "unpublishable." Gertrude Stein would never have said that. She always had a fondness for him. And what really matters is not the pettiness and rivalry and spite at the end but the open, fond hearts and the true affection at the start. There was nothing small or mean about Gertrude Stein or Ernest Hemingway. Each one has testified specifically to love and respect for the other. Nothing can change that.

Robert Coates was a rue de Fleurus favorite. A tall, red-headed aspiring novelist, he later became art critic for *The New Yorker* magazine. Glenway Wescott, best known for his novel *The Grandmothers,* paid his respects. The poet William Carlos Williams came dutifully and left, it might be said, indifferently. Williams was too deeply rooted in his native soil to admire transplanted Americans like Gertrude Stein or her friend Natalie Clifford Barney. Williams' own particular friend, Ezra Pound, was a caller. Pound liked Gertrude Stein and her work more than she ever managed to like him. Paul Robeson, the great singer and actor, was an *habitué* of the rue de Fleurus *soirées*. At this time began the important friendship with Carl Van Vechten. In the early 1920's Van Vechten already had a reputation as a witty and perceptive critic of music and ballet. He was also attracting attention as a novelist. From his first reading of *The Portrait of Mabel Dodge at the Villa Curonia* he had been an enthusiastic Stein convert.

English admirers, also, flocked to the Stein-Toklas Saturday evenings. Among them were Edith Sitwell, the poet; Lady Ottoline Morrell, patroness of the arts; Roger Fry, the art critic; John Lane, and many others. Another expatriate, the poet T. S. Eliot, came over from London. He was editing a magazine, *The Criterion*. It professed to be interested in the new and different. He looked forward, he solemnly informed Gertrude Stein, to the privilege of printing something of hers. But he insisted it must be her newest work. He had no sooner left than she sat down and wrote "The Fifteenth of November." That was the date of his visit. Presumably it was mailed to him the sixteenth. The date and title proved not to matter much in the long run. Eliot published it only after a delay of more than a year. Alfred Kreymborg, the poet, also about to edit a new magazine, *Broom*, stopped to see what Gertrude Stein had to contribute. She had enough to fill his proposed publication for years. He settled finally for one small item.

Bernard Faÿ, who would later translate some Stein into French, was a frequent guest. About this time Jacques Lipschitz and Jo Davidson sculptured her and Francis Picabia did a portrait. The sculptures and the painting were no match for the Picasso masterpiece. Just the same, the in-

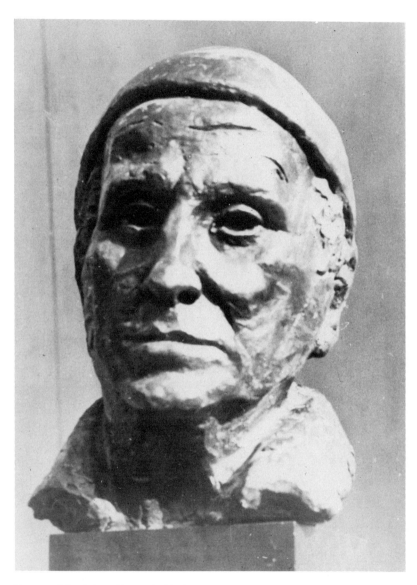

Jacques Lipschitz, *Gertrude Stein.*

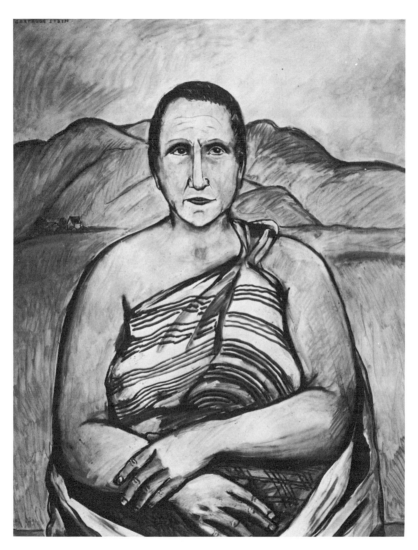

Francis Picabia, *Gertrude Stein.*

terest of these artists was another measure of her growing literary stature.

The association now beginning with Sylvia Beach was invaluable. Miss Beach had indulged in various adventures while trying to decide on a career. She settled on a bookstore. Situated in the rue de l'Odéon not far from the Luxembourg Gardens, it was called Shakespeare and Company. Gertrude Stein became a faithful customer and was the first to sign up in this famous store's lending library. Later Miss Beach would publish James Joyce's *Ulysses*. The novel *Ulysses* would pioneer as boldly as Gertrude Stein's *The Making of Americans*. Gertrude Stein did not like rivals. Most writers don't. Yet she didn't let Miss Beach's backing of Joyce affect her own close and enduring ties with the bookstore.

13 *To put into a book what is to be read in a book. . . .*

—LUCY CHURCH AMIABLY

During the 1920's Gertrude Stein's work was perhaps at its most unfathomable. She never before and never afterward was any more successful at making her writing a puzzle. One result was a growing clique of admirers. It was a time of experimental writing; artists, too, and also architects and composers were experimenting. Gertrude Stein's work was not so varied as Picasso's yet it included a fairly wide range of pioneering ventures. She made demands on words no one had ever made before. Some readers found a sort of magic in her novel arrangements. Some probed for hidden meanings. Some took pleasure in furnishing glosses or translations. Some read her, admittedly, as a fad because reading her was popular in select circles. Some regarded her work as songlike. One young man, though this was later in New York, memorized pages and pages and gave Stein "recitals." In general it was agreed that her original, unique writing was an unprecedented expansion of the potentialities of the English language.

A second result of the sometimes impenetrable quality of her prose was that her admirers, however enthusiastic, were few. They were so few that commercial publication was impractical. Consequently Miss Toklas founded Plain Edition. The name was suggested by Gertrude Stein. The venture was financed by the sale of a painting and probably also by some Toklas money. The sole purpose was the publication of Gertrude Stein manuscripts.

The best known and most deserving of the privately printed works was *Lucy Church Amiably*. The copy on my desk is a lot the worse for wear. The sharp, piercing blue of the binding has been rubbed white on the edges. On the front, exactly as on the title page, a large GERTRUDE STEIN stands at the top. The conventional plug for the contents reads, "A Novel of Romantic beauty and nature and which Looks Like an Engraving" (the capitalization abides by no known rules). Next comes the title, LUCY CHURCH AMIABLY. In lower case under it the epigraph reads, "And with a nod she turned her head toward the falling water. Amiably." Finally we learn that this is a FIRST EDITION. The printer is identified: "Paris Imprimerie Union 13, Rue Méchain, 13 1930." On the back this information is provided: "Price: Three Dollars." Opposite the title page is the explanation: "The plain Edition an Edition of first Editions of all the work not yet Printed of Gertrude Stein."

This project was a formidable task. Gertrude Stein was

used to making editorial decisions. Miss Toklas was not used to the ways of business. Copy had to be prepared professionally, a printing shop and a bindery found, contracts signed, and the finished product marketed. The financial risk was enormous. The two women would not have run such chances if they had not been absolutely convinced of the quality of their product. The costs may have been ridiculously low compared to today's. Yet the available funds were ridiculously low, too. As far as I know there was never any reliable accounting. Nevertheless the businesswomen must have lost a lot of money. Yet their books today are worth many times their original investment.

The second choice for publication by Plain Edition was *Before the Flowers of Friendship Faded Friendship Faded*. The title has the smart appearance of being a repetition while in fact amounting to two different statements. It was written on the occasion of a misunderstanding with a French poet. Georges Hugnet had translated some Stein prose into French. She in turn translated a poem of his into English. The trouble was, he complained, that she took as much credit for the work as she gave him, and at his resentment friendship faded.

The publication date of . . . *Friendship Faded Friendship Faded* was 1931. A front page dates *Lucy Church Amiably* 1931, too, though the novel itself bears the date 1930. Late in 1931 there appeared a third work, *How to Write*. This more professional print job was done in Maurice Darantière's press at Dijon. It was Darantière who printed *The Making of Americans* and also Joyce's *Ulysses*. Thus he had benefited by some invaluable experience. He had worked not only in a foreign language but in that language in its most enigmatic forms.

In 1932 Darantière printed *Operas and Plays*, physically the most attractive product of the Toklas enterprise. It totals four hundred pages but they and the type, also, are small. Bound in paper and boxed, it had a first . . . and last . . . printing of five hundred copies. This was a more realistic estimate of sales possibilities than the one thousand copies of *How to Write*. The aggressive members of the firm (we may designate them editor and business manager) themselves sallied out as salesmen. They left copies at Shakespeare and Company, at the shop of a friend of Sylvia Beach's, and in many of the other bookstores that are spread so wonderfully all over Paris. Then Gertrude Stein walked back to these places to gaze fondly and admiringly at her work on display. Other authors share her desire to see their names on their books out where thousands of other people can see, too.

Operas and Plays contained several works destined to be seen and heard as well as read. The best known was *Four Saints in Three Acts*. The composer Virgil Thomson later made this into an actual opera with music, staging, scenery, performers and even, joy of joys, an audience—in fact scores of audiences. The table of contents lists the well-known "Capital Capitals," also set to music by Thomson. Another gem in *Operas and Plays* bears the title "They Must. Be Wedded. To Their Wife." Written in 1931, this would develop into an entrancing ballet. You could do anything with a Stein work, though some obdurate critics complained you just couldn't read it.

Lucy Church Amiably . . . "Price: Three Dollars" is about the finest, most characteristic Stein of this period. It opens with an "Advertisement" of some fifteen or twenty lines. Then comes "Begins the Middle of May Introduction." This totals some thirty-five pages. At last we reach the body of this "Novel of Romantic beauty . . . which Looks Like an Engraving." Lucy is a place made into a person. The town of Lucey was not far from the summer home of Gertrude Stein. But it was Lucey with an *e*, not Lucy. Accuracy was not overly important either in spelling or in larger matters . . . not to this author. Other proper names are sprinkled here and there in the text. They serve to pin the picture down, they orient the landscape. They are related to the direction signs on a map . . . North South East West. Or they fulfill the same prosaic purpose as the actual newspaper clipping or cardboard ticket pasted on a Cubist collage. The painter measured the reality of his brushwork against the real print. The writer measured her fancy against the facts. *Lucy Church Amiably* names Alice Babette, or Miss Toklas; Alphonse Lamartine, the poet, and Anthelme Brillat-Savarin, the epicure, both nineteenth-century figures; and Paul Claudel, the contemporary poet and playwright. They were all associated with the Lucey-Bilignin-Aix-Chambéry axis. Some towns are listed, too: Chambéry, a resort center, and Grenoble, with its university. Mont Blanc, highest of the Alps, rates a mention.

Part of the fiction was fact only slightly disguised. Gertrude Stein took what was right under her nose and put it right under her nose on paper. All writers find in environment and acquaintances much or most of the material for their novels. In Gertrude Stein the connection was sometimes easily discovered, sometimes concealed. In *Lucy Church Amiably* there was a clear transferal from experience to book.

Gertrude Stein loved Paris but liked to be in the country in the summer. This on a different scale reflects her love for America but her liking to be in France. She knew southern France intimately. She enjoyed being in the sun, too. During the war she had been stationed near the Mediterranean. She had spent many peacetime months in Spain, in Italy and in France's Saint-Rémy among more Roman ruins. She patronized the Hotel Pernollet in Belley in the department of Ain. A French *département* is a larger unit than an American county but smaller than an American state. Ain lies on the Swiss frontier. Gertrude Stein and her companion were living in the Hotel Pernollet when they took on the blinding task of correcting proofs of *The Making of Americans*. The hotel is a favorite among gourmets. Among its patrons were or would be the duke of Windsor and his American friend Wallis Warfield Simpson.

Gertrude Stein now owned another car. This was christened Godiva. The eleventh-century Lady Godiva was distressed by the onerous taxes laid on the people by her tyrannical husband. All right, he bargained with her, he would not exact another penny if she would ride naked through the marketplace. It was a strange proposition from a husband but she took him up on it. The new Ford was sort of naked, too. It came with not much more than wheels, motor and seats. But it safely transported the women all through Ain. One day in the distance they spotted a

Alice B. Toklas and Gertrude Stein in "Godiva," 1927.

gabled and terraced house. Even from afar it looked like just the country place they dreamed of. Without getting any closer, they made inquiries. A French army lieutenant lived there. Stationed in Ain, he needed a home in the region. The Americans made discreet moves. Could they get him promoted or transferred? Whether or not their efforts were influential, he was posted to North Africa.

That was a few years later but the women had been patient. Now they moved in and for the first time saw close-up the property they had rented. The wall and narrow gate at the back were separated from the house by scrub growth. A central hall led from back to front. The kitchen and laundry were to the right; the dining room, living room and a flight of stairs to the left. The second floor was allotted to three or four bedrooms and a spacious square bathroom. There was a splendid view toward the Alps and Italy. Plants and graveled walks made a formal garden of the terrace. At the far edge a low stone wall marked where the ground dropped away sharply. With square, tiled toolhouses at each end, it stretched the width of the lot. Lizards flitted about on it in the sun.

There was always one servant, sometimes two. For a while it was an Indochinese named Trac. He had connections with a place whose name we know too well: Saigon. Some furniture in the house had belonged to Brillat-Savarin. During World War II the lieutenant, now promoted to captain, moved back and insisted on reoccupying the building. The women were ousted but Bilignin was always close to their hearts.

The story of the lieutenant and Bilignin figures in *Lucy*

122

Gertrude Stein with Mrs. Rogers and the dogs Basket and Pepe, in the garden at Bilignin.

Church Amiably. But mostly it is a novel not of what happened ("I believe I do not like anything that happens," Gertrude Stein once said) but a novel of what was. It was accurately publicized as having "Romantic beauty." The pages reproduce or re-create the peace and solitude of isolated Lucey village and its church with one tower inexplicably onion-shaped. There are occasional intriguingly short chapters:

CHAPTER XXIX
There are two ways two a day. Two days.
Come again.

Or to come again:

CHAPTER XLVIII
Lucy Church was obstinate.

The longer passages are typical Gertrude Stein. Every now and then she inveigles you into thinking a sentence is veering off north or east, south or west, or perhaps coming to an end. Or she inveigles you into expecting a specific meaning and form as in the time-honored, ordinary sentence. Her pregnant starts, but false-pregnant starts, tease you. Does she, doesn't she, mean to go here, go there? Collections of the sentences resemble clusters of Fourth of July rockets. You never know where the fiery offshoots will go until they do go. I like this unexpectedness, this unpredictability. We are so used to sentences accompanied by signs pointing unmistakably this way and that way only. What is so exciting as untried and uncharted directions? Gertrude Stein knows what she is doing, too. She knows you expect her sentences to follow the trail blazed in the course of centuries. But what's wrong with going her way? she asks. Why do we insist on a conventional progression in prosaic and humdrum sentences?

This is not "useful" writing. Gertrude Stein claimed in another connection that masterpieces are not necessary. *Lucy Church Amiably* is not necessary. It doesn't get you anywhere, it has no money value for you. Yet paradoxically it is priceless. *Lucy Church Amiably* is purely for *Lucy Church Amiably's* own sake.

There is one outright Stein jibe: "To put into a book what is to be read in a book, bits of information and tender feeling." Then she continues laughing a bit sharply at us:

124

"How do you like your two percent bits of information and tender feeling?" The effect of all this is not a symphony but a tone poem. Gertrude Stein never meant to communicate tender feeling or information. She was interested in mood, aura and ambiance, in the envelope. Her words form a sort of halo around the ordinary, tangible, stuffy reality. She sublimates the fact and in her elusive way hits right on the truth. Natalie Clifford Barney, Gertrude Stein's friend and author of several volumes of aphorisms, said that she herself liked to drive straight at a point, whereas Gertrude Stein, it seemed to her, liked to avoid the point and aim all around it.

Gertrude Stein possessed a unique skill as a word trainer. At her command words stood on their hind paws, lay down and rolled over, balanced balls on their noses, jumped through hoops. They did anything but play dead. Yet she was no martinet, she was fond of words. "I like anything that a word can do," she wrote. And again she claimed, "I like the feeling of words doing as they want to do." Her mastery is demonstrated best in a few shorter pieces. Take, for instance, "A Valentine to Sherwood Anderson. Idem the Same." It appeared in *Portraits and Prayers*. One section reads:

> Very fine is my Valentine.
> Very fine and very mine.
> Very mine is my valentine very mine and very fine.
> Very fine is my valentine and mine, very fine very mine and mine is my valentine.

This utterly charming poem is alive with the valentine spirit. It proclaims gaily and happily, "I love you I love you." It is as possessive as true love tends to be. It also is confident.

"I love you," it says but also, "I know you love me." The words do not add up in conventional grammatical terms to any usual sense. Nevertheless here is the expansive, embracing valentine spirit. If your fellow or girl mailed you this, you'd be tickled. It has a kind of magic. It gets under your skin. It is not mere tender feeling but passionate feeling. Another work, also dated 1932, is a companion piece. Its subject is the French composer Erik Satie. With his name as title it begins:

> Erik Satie benignly.
> Come to Sylvia do.
> Sylvia Sybil and Sarah
> A bird is for more cookcoo.
> And then what spreads thinner, and a letter. It is
> early for all.

This is the way it was written, or at least printed—spelling, punctuation and all. It possesses precisely the wit and sprightliness characteristic of Satie's music. He served as the mentor of "Les Six," a group of six modernist composers. You don't take the poem word by word or syllable by syllable. You don't take Satie's music note by note, either. The correct total effect comes in a quick lilting reading. It is merry and in a way imitative. This is Erik Satie music translated in verse. A song substitutes for a portrait. You might indeed accuse Satie of borrowing . . . I would not say ideas . . . but titles from Gertrude Stein. About ten years her senior, he was composing while she was writing. Among his titles are "Sketches and Annoyances of a Wooden Manikin" and "Three Pieces in the Shape of a Pear."

126

14 *Really there is no use in going to see a thing if you have not written it no use at all.*

—EVERYBODY'S AUTOBIOGRAPHY

The most important composer in Gertrude Stein's life was Virgil Thomson. Entering his thirties around 1930, he had been first a student and then a teacher at Harvard. For some years he had been studying in Paris with the well-known Nadia Boulanger. Small and lively, he bubbled over with ideas. Physically he resembled rather the spry Miss Toklas than the Buddha-like Gertrude Stein. He had written music for some of her short pieces. Influenced by Satie, his elder by some years, Thomson wanted to do a Gertrude Stein opera. It was the beginning of a long collaboration, which was broken only briefly because of some problems connected with a contract. But the difficulties were patched up and forgotten in the extraordinary success of their joint venture.

The libretto provided by Gertrude Stein was *Four Saints in Three Acts*. It was first published in *transition* magazine in 1929. Then it appeared in the Plain Edition *Operas and Plays* of 1932 and was brought out separately by Random House in 1934. That was the year of the opera's premiere in the United States.

Though book publishers were cool to Gertrude Stein, the editors of "little magazines" were beginning to welcome her. Sometimes they paid a pittance. Eugene Jolas, principal activator of *transition*, the best known and most influential magazine, paid modestly thanks to funds supplied by his wife, Maria. The *Little Review*, published in Chicago by Margaret Anderson and Jane Heap, paid nothing. Harriet Monroe's *Poetry* in the same city gave modest fees. Robert Frost, James Joyce, Ezra Pound, Carl Sandburg, Gertrude Stein and many others appeared in one or the other of these Chicago outlets. We have noted *The Criterion* in London. *This Quarter* was published in Paris right around the corner from the Dôme and the Rotonde, cafés popular with the writers who contributed to it. Somewhat later Italy would produce *Botteghe Oscure* with an American sponsor, and New York turned out *New Directions* and *Cross-Section*.

If Gertrude Stein's audience was small, it was beyond question discerning, informed and distinguished. The cognoscenti and the intelligentsia read her. The lucky man in the street was about to make her acquaintance. Her great big wonderful years were 1933, 1934 and 1935. In the fall of 1933 came *The Autobiography of Alice B. Toklas*. *Four Saints in Three Acts* premiered in 1934. In that year and for a few months in 1935 Gertrude Stein made a triumphal tour of her native land.

Let's attend the opera first. Chronologically it comes second yet that would interrupt the tale of her book, her tour and her later works. *Four Saints in Three Acts* opened on February 8, 1934 . . . a cold, snowy night. The Friends and Enemies of Modern Music sponsored it in the Avery Memorial Theatre of the Hartford (Connecticut) Atheneum, that is, the Hartford museum. Then it moved to New York for a short run on Broadway. It was performed in Chicago just in time for the librettist to see it during her American tour. It also went on radio and was heard in concert halls.

It was Thomson who decided on an all-Negro cast. Florine Stettheimer designed the airiest, gayest cellophane scenery and fanciful, elaborate costumes. She made a fairyland of it. Maurice Grosser prepared the text for the stage. The score was a completely delightful match for the spirit and form of the text. Musical themes, repetitions and developments perfectly fitted the libretto's mystifying idiosyncrasies. Thomson divined exactly how to create the musical setting to parallel the unique words.

Opening night was a social as well as cultural event. It was black tie . . . I was there. Perhaps Gertrude Stein, aristocratic but at the same time democratic, would not have approved of this chichi aspect. She had had mostly a select and élite audience but that was not her fault and not her preference. She believed she was not exclusively highbrow. She was confident she had an appeal for the masses. Years later she canceled the performance of a play of hers in an army camp because it had been scheduled for officers only. Even so, the high-society feature of the Hartford show was effective publicity. It would have been a mistake to object. Above all, the sophisticated audience was understanding

129

A scene from the premiere of *Four Saints in Three Acts*, Hartford, Connecticut, 1934.

and sympathetic. Every seat was taken, lots of people were turned away.

The opera, while a milestone, was also perhaps a dead end. It enjoyed only short runs. It did little to influence the musical stage . . . though Stein's writing had many imitators. But the actual performance was an electrifying experience. You didn't just like it, you loved it.

Four Saints in Three Acts promised a lot that it did not deliver. It also delivered a lot that it did not promise. There were four acts instead of three and fifteen saints instead of four. The chief roles were sung by Edward Matthews, Beatrice Robinson Wayne, Bruce Howard, Altonall Hines and Abner Dorsey. They did not have immortal voices but what they did have was perhaps better: fervor and enthusiasm. Dedicated, impassioned and zestful, they threw themselves into the show with gusto. They benefited greatly, too, from Thomson's painstaking coaching. The opera was solemn, ecstatic, religious, fast-paced, colorful, tuneful. It was both nostalgic and avant-garde. It opened thus:

> To know to know to love her so.
> Four saints prepare for saints.

Soon came a stage direction: "Repeat First Act." Thomson wittily set it and other stage directions to music and they were sung. He worked in total harmony with the insouciant spirit of the libretto. "How many saints are there in it" was a frequent refrain. The question made sense because at first hearing or even second you were not sure of the answer.

Gertrude Stein doted on that "how many" interrogation. One reason was her particular delight in playing with strings of numbers. "How many days are there in it" . . . "How many houses are there in it" . . . "How many eggs are there in it" . . . "How many no doubt are there of it" all come from *Lucy Church Amiably*. In *Four Saints* you hear or read "How many nails are there in it" and "How many Acts are there in it" . . . again a hard one to answer at first. In *Four in America* she asked, "How many acts are there in moving." The rhythm of the phrase and the monotony of it fascinated her. Besides she was always a questioner, though she never bothered with question marks.

The Spanish visit of Gertrude Stein and Miss Toklas had inspired the text . . . it is not irrelevant that years later Miss Toklas became a Catholic convert. Miss Toklas so loved Ávila that she would have liked to settle there within the old walls. Gertrude Stein would not have dreamed of abandoning Paris. The saints in the text, the author explained in an American lecture, were the landscape. Landscape, we remember, was a favorite subject. She reveled in the setting, the ambiance, the variety of surroundings. Among other phrases of hers that have persisted are "Pigeons on the grass alas," "It makes it well fish," "If a magpie in the sky on the sky can not cry." You see these magpies today outlined as black and white crosses against the Spanish sky. There was another religious connotation, Gertrude Stein said. Flattened unnaturally, with no depth, they resembled birds in primitive paintings of the Annunciation and other sacred subjects.

"There is a difference between Barcelona and Avila," she wrote. It is certainly the truth. Then she went on: "There is a difference between Barcelona" . . . period. The opera ended:

Last Act.
Which is a fact.

Gertrude Stein started to write the opera under brandnew conditions. For once she could count on a reader, an adapter and best of all an audience. To be sure she professed to write solely for herself or "for myself and strangers." But let anyone breathe a hint of some specified purpose and she immediately reached for her pen. Thus in her opera she produced a lively, rhythmic, animated, often baffling, always intriguing opus. It was a landscape just as much as *Lucy Church Amiably* was a landscape.

Does she mean what she says when she describes saints as landscapes? Or *Lucy Church* as landscape? Do you see what she means, or hear what she means? Does reading the text or hearing the opera give a landscape effect? I think so. Maybe the correct view is that in its presence you feel vaguely and ambiguously in the presence of a landscape. What is a landscape but an ambiance, or, abstractly speaking, a sensation? Matisse once hoped to make a painting as comfortable as an armchair. Gertrude Stein's writing was as intrusive, as permeating, as present as a landscape. You don't measure, judge, define, look at or listen to it. Instead it is something into which to sink, on which to float. You surrender to an impression of well-being. The significance of a work directed not at sense but at the senses is baffling and elusive. Gertrude Stein doesn't use words in the age-old context to create her effects, so it is difficult to use such words to describe her effects. Yet commensurable effects there are.

A lot of people, of course, fight it. No, I won't, they declare—take it away! Since it looks mad, it must be mad. The only approach is to relax, to yield. You make your mind a blank and let the Stein prose register as weather registers on a barometer. A decade after this performance the New York publisher William R. Scott brought out one of Gertrude Stein's rare children's books. It is called *The World Is*

Round. The publisher's suggestion about reading it, printed on the jacket flap, applies to grown-up Stein prose, too: "This book was written to be enjoyed. It is meant to be read aloud a few chapters at a time. . . . Don't bother about the commas which aren't there, read the words. Don't worry about the sense that is there, read the words faster. If you have any trouble read faster and faster until you don't." Then he repeated his opening statement: "This book was written to be enjoyed."

Gertrude Stein wrote serious, thought-provoking books about her calling, about herself. They are not to be taken lightly. *The Making of Americans, Three Lives,* the six lectures delivered on the American tour and *The Geographical History of America,* among others, were not aimed just to entertain. But much of the rest of her writing proves that she liked living and wanted you to share that liking. Pleasantness, satisfaction, contentment are registered time and again.

Another work of this period abounds in the same carefree spirit. "They Must. Be Wedded. To Their Wife" is dated 1931. With the title changed to "A Wedding Bouquet," this was made into a ballet. The choreography was by Frederick Ashton, later Sir Frederick. The music was by Gerald Berners (Lord Berners), who also designed the costumes and decor. The interpretation on the dance floor was freer than that of *Four Saints* on the operatic stage. It was premiered in London in the old Sadler's Wells Theatre on April 27, 1937. Constant Lambert conducted. The Sadler's Wells Ballet Company, later to be promoted to The Royal Ballet and moved to Covent Garden, eventually brought the charming production to New York. Ninette de Valois, the company's *grande dame*, played the part of Daniel Webster. Margot Fonteyn, one of the age's great ballerinas, was Julia. Robert Helpmann was the bridegroom and Michael Somes was Guy. One character in the libretto was Pepe, Miss Toklas' pint-sized hairless Chihuahua. He got into the ballet, too, danced by Joyce Farron. It was a distinguished cast.

Program notes quoted Gertrude Stein phrases to define the characters and set the mood. Julia herself was "known as forlorn." Of the dog it was said, "Little dogs resemble little girls." The reference to the bridegroom was "They all speak as if they expected him not to be charming." The Four Guests were thus identified: "They incline to oblige only one when they pair." The pauses and broken rhythms in the text suggested timing or beat and the nature of the dance steps.

Gertrude Stein and Miss Toklas went to London for the premiere. The author was very happy to take a bow. She enjoyed herself immensely. She wrote later, "Really there is no use in going to see a thing if you have not written it no use at all."

By now she was becoming familiar with London and the English. Besides the two trips just before World War I, there had been some since. In 1926 she had lectured at both Cambridge and Oxford universities. At the suggestion of invitations, her immediate response had been an emphatic no. The very idea gave her stage fright. Edith Sitwell intervened. Gertrude Stein had already written a portrait of the English author called "Sitwell Edith Sitwell." She wanted

135

Gertrude Stein to come to England and stand up for herself. Two ancient universities urged her to accept their invitations. Edith Sitwell was not at all complimentary to them in advocating the trip. She argued, "It is quite undoubted that a personality does help to convince half-intelligent people." It is true that personal appearances help book sales. So Gertrude Stein decided to expose herself to these "half-intelligent" audiences in England's most prestigious seats of learning. First she had to get some tips on lecturing. One consultant advised her to hold her head up and hardly ever look down at her paper. The second one said she should turn her head down, with her eyes on her text, and hardly ever look up at her audience.

She managed handsomely. After she delivered her set lecture, she submitted to questioning from the floor. She had feared heckling but the approach was serious. She wound up, indeed, with a triumph. A statement of hers was challenged. She had said . . . holding her head up or tipping it down . . . that everything was the same and everything was different. How could that be? she was asked. By a lucky chance the same question was asked by two different men in different parts of the hall. Her ready answer was that the paired questions proved it . . . alike and different, too. She got a laugh and applause.

15 *I have no inclination to be scolded.*

—BEE TIME VINE

Gertrude Stein enjoyed a strange immunity to violence. Two wars raged around her. Rioting erupted in Paris streets. She remained unscathed. In her immediate neighborhood she also carried on behind a protective shield. In Bilignin lightning struck but never struck her. A friend, Madame Pernollet, fell to her death from a window in the family's famed hotel. Presumably it was suicide but it was not explained to Gertrude Stein's satisfaction. Tragedy befell a trio of women in a nearby chateau. One was found with two bullets in her head. Again the verdict was, mysteriously, suicide. Gertrude Stein used to lead her visitors on a walk through the chateau grounds . . . here it happened, there the body was found.

Perhaps the fact that she was so busy explains her immunity. There was an almost unnatural aloofness about her.

137

She gave her mind to essentials. She could shut her mind tight against the ephemeral. "It takes a lot of time to be a genius," she claimed. A person had to hang around, had to loiter. He had to let ideas, as is said of a salad, marinate. People have accused her of being lazy. If her aim was fame and glory, if her aim was to rack up works of so-called genius, she was one of the hardest workers of her time. Any writer can look like a loiterer to the uninformed. Often the hard work is done before the writer picks up a pen. Just lying fallow can wear a man out. One of the finest novels of our century came from a man who looked and acted the fatuous dilettante: Marcel Proust. Everything Gertrude Stein did fed into her art. She was a giant hopper of experiences. It was emptied daily on her tabletop and covered it all over.

She wrote on scraps of paper. She wrote in the lined notebooks in which French schoolchildren write their compositions. She was a helter-skelter writer. There was nothing neat about Gertrude Stein at work. If it was hard sometimes to understand what she meant when you could read it, there was a still harder earlier stage. Her wild, undisciplined scrawl was hard to make out. The Kiddies used to take turns deciphering her letters. First one peered at the page close-up and then one held it way off. It could be as impenetrable as the code of a spy.

Somehow the scraps of paper and notebooks never got lost. Someone manned a typewriter and transcribed them legibly. It might be Ernest Hemingway, or Miss Toklas, or that obliging Baltimore friend Etta Cone. Allowing for a discouraging lapse of time, it all got printed, too. Gertrude Stein said it took six weeks to write *The Autobiography of*

Alice B. Toklas. She could cover ground fast when the spirit moved. Once in a while you can measure her pace when she unwittingly drops a hint. New Year's is mentioned within a few pages of a reference to Christmas . . . so there is a week's output. Normally she seems to have spent half an hour a day with pen in hand. The rest of the time things germinated.

She was of course no finicky, piddling writer. She aimed at big effects. She believed in getting everything down. She was never willing to settle for less than that, either. There was practically no editing, no correcting and little cutting. When Miss Toklas typed she might presume to alter a word or two. Or maybe she misread. But the changes were minor. What came from the horse's mouth must not be tampered with. Everything Gertrude Stein wrote was in her opinion as good as everything else she wrote. One page is as good as the next is as good as the next is as good as the next.

Success was sudden, like striking oil. After prospecting for years and years, she hit a gusher. It absolutely delighted her. Hardly anyone ever relished fame as Gertrude Stein did. Hardly any writer ever had it laid on so thick, either. Her success began with one tart, witty, zestful book, *The Autobiography of Alice B. Toklas.* It was a book everyone could understand. She did what she had not done before: made her prose plain and available to the man in the street. An American publisher gave her a sly dig on this score. If her writing had made sense earlier, he said, she would have won all this renown earlier. She had a prompt, sharp retort. If she was famous, she declared, it was not because of what people could understand but because of what they could not. The puzzle was what got the publicity. Solutions were of minor general interest.

In Bilignin in October and November 1932, she wrote *The Autobiography of Alice B. Toklas*. Its success in 1933 helped advertise the Hartford performance of *Four Saints in Three Acts* in 1934. First had come decades of writing that sometimes could not be read even through a glass darkly. Then she turned the tables on the public. She dropped the mystification. She reverted to the simplicity of *Three Lives*. She wrote the King's English and Everyman's English. While keeping all her old audience, she picked up a vast new one. The new style could be parsed, it was punctuated, it had "Capital Capitals." It did make sense . . . which is not to concede that the rest of her writing did not. While Everyman doted on the Toklas *Autobiography*, it was followed appropriately by *Everybody's Autobiography*.

The Toklas *Autobiography* was of course written by Gertrude Stein, though the confession of authorship comes only at the end. There we are told that she had kept urging Miss Toklas to write. "Just think," she would say, "what a lot of money you would make." Gertrude Stein invented titles: *My Life with the Great, Wives of Geniuses I Have Sat With, My Twenty-five Years With Gertrude Stein.* Finally running out of patience, according to the closing paragraph, "Gertrude Stein said, it does not look to me as if you were going to write that autobiography. You know what I am going to do. I am going to write it for you. I am going to write it as simply as Defoe did the autobiography of Robinson Crusoe. And she has and this is it."

On the very last page we get the last of the book's

sixteen illustrations. It is a reproduction of the first page of the manuscript. It is not Miss Toklas' writing, fine and precise like an etching. It is instead the writing of Gertrude Stein, flowing, free, loose like a lithograph.

The obvious mystification about the authorship was perhaps just a game intended to intrigue the public. But there was a precedent. Early in her career Gertrude Stein had thought of using the pseudonym Jane Sands. Now, understandably, she borrowed Alice B. Toklas. The Paris Left Bank in the first decades of this century has been the subject of countless biographies, memoirs, histories and studies. The best of them all is *The Autobiography of Alice B. Toklas* . . . entertaining, perceptive, enthusiastic, sympathetic, provocative. It is free of malice but that is not to deny its abundance of cutting, dry wit and pointed comment.

Some irreverent Stein critics have suggested it was written by Miss Toklas. I once implied as much myself. But I didn't mean it. It is from start to finish pure Stein. The illustration of the handwriting and the concluding statement are not the only proofs. The determining factor is the text itself. Gertrude Stein was Gertrude Stein. However fond you were of Miss Toklas, she could not hold a candle to her companion. After Gertrude Stein's death Miss Toklas wrote her own autobiography, really her own. It is called *What Is Remembered*. She remembered many things already related in the original Toklas *Autobiography*.

The differences are remarkable. Miss Toklas wrote well but in an academic manner. Her book showed that she had been to school as clearly as that she had lived in Paris. Ger-

The first page of the manuscript of *The Autobiography of Alice B. Toklas*. (Courtesy, Random House, Inc.)

trude Stein somehow captured the spirit of the time and place. She made those years come alive. Miss Toklas merely recorded them. Gertrude Stein may often have been wrong. Indeed she was angrily accused of it. I'm sure Miss Toklas got her facts right, her "two percent bits of information." Even Leo Stein would have approved of the Toklas account . . . and Miss Toklas would have hated that.

Each one, for instance, offers her version of the famous Rousseau banquet. It took place just after Miss Toklas arrived in Paris. The painter Henri Rousseau, whose checkered career included a job as customs collector (hence, his nickname, "Le Douanier"), would have starved to death if he had had to depend on the money his art brought in. After his death his pictures, created out of an astounding, primitive, naive vision, became highly prized—one recently sold for a quarter of a million dollars. That would have stunned him, and those who had assembled, as they claimed, to honor him, simply wouldn't have believed it. Though they talked of honoring him, what they planned was merely a bang-up good time. Picasso had just acquired a new Rousseau canvas. Fernande Olivier, Picasso's friend, decided to celebrate with a feast. She hired a caterer. She invited Gertrude and Leo Stein and their visitor, Miss Toklas.

The party began at a café at the foot of the steep rue Ravignan. When the Americans arrived, the festivities were already turning rowdy. Marie Laurencin, the painter friend of Guillaume Apollinaire, was tipsy. The crowd walked, stumbled and staggered uphill to the *Bateau Lavoir*. André Salmon, Braque, and colorful characters from the neighborhood joined in the fun. Rousseau was seated in a special

143

chair that served as a throne. The sign "Honneur à Rousseau" was hung over his head. He promptly fell asleep. Everyone else made merry. Someone delivered a speech in praise of the guest of honor. Someone did a dance. Someone sang. Miss Toklas, understood to be fresh from the American Wild West, was invited to sing a song about the great wide plains. She declined. It was like a scene from *La Vie de Bohème*. Mimi, Musetta, Rodolfo and Marcello were absent and there was no hint of the music Puccini composed. But it was a carefree, happy Bohemian night—drinking, laughing, antic.

Gertrude Stein's book made it that kind of an affair: noisy, boisterous, vagabond, giddy and slightly wild and slightly crazy. You read her and you are there, too, just as if you yourself had tossed down a few glasses of wine. Miss Toklas wrote about it all excellently but by comparison more coldly. The spirit eluded her. In the Toklas *Autobiography*, as we have noted, she claimed that "a bell within me rang" upon encountering three geniuses: Stein, Picasso and Whitehead. No bell quite rang for Miss Toklas herself. Leo wrote that "Art, however, is not what we say *about* anything. It is what we say." Gertrude Stein's account was art.

Leo acknowledged . . . not grudgingly, either . . . a certain comic flair in his sister's book. But he blamed her for a lot of inaccuracies. She claimed she had done things that in reality, he said, he alone had done. His complaints concerned largely the acquisition of their modern paintings. "What a liar she is!" he would exclaim.

Literature cannot be judged on the basis of accuracy and

inaccuracy. It is not mathematics or science. It can err in details or indeed in major respects and still remain literature. There again the art is not what we say about a thing, it is what we say. We do not read *The Autobiography of Alice B. Toklas* for the sake of finding out when the first Picasso was bought by whom for how much. We do find out, better than anywhere else, what it meant to buy that first Picasso. We learn what it meant to live in the creative whirlwind that was Paris in the 1910's and 1920's. We learn what it meant to commit oneself to the modernist cause. Gertrude Stein once pointed out to the Kiddie the importance of owning a picture. Argue for a work on a museum wall and you argue theoretically. Your opinion alone is at stake. Buy the picture, put your good money into it and you put yourself on the spot. You have to admit you're committed. You have to defend that commitment. It's not a matter of pretending to take sides but of really taking sides. That was part of the thrill and excitement of daringly buying moderns in Paris sixty or seventy years ago.

Leo was not the only one to criticize. Over the years the most positive, the rudest, rebuffs had come from New York and London and Paris editors. Gertrude Stein was used to criticism by readers who claimed they couldn't understand her. All of a sudden she came under a barrage of attacks from people who understood her clearly.

The core of the opposition consisted, unhappily, of some of her formerly enthusiastic supporters. The "little magazine" that had built her up now was bent on pulling her down. Eugene and Maria Jolas of *transition* jumped on her with both feet, or all four. Jolas himself was one of the boldest experimenters in an abstruse language he called Vertigralism. He had become a particular partisan of James Joyce's writing, which could be as baffling as Gertrude Stein's. He published a lot of Joyce; in effect his work replaced the contributions of Miss Stein, who had been introduced to the magazine by Elliot Paul, serving as part-time editor. She didn't like that. Jolas' feelings cooled, or heated, when she gave, in his opinion, too much credit to Paul and too little to himself and Madame Jolas for publishing her. They rallied their friends to launch a counterattack. The title was "Testimony Against Gertrude Stein." The fifteen-page pamphlet was issued in February 1935 as a supplement to *transition*.

A handful of contributors one by one retorted to this or that comment. Madame Jolas indignantly claimed that her husband's role as the magazine's "director and intellectual *animateur*" had been ignored. Braque said Gertrude Stein "understood nothing of what went on around her." André Salmon agreed: "What incomprehension of an epoch!" He also denied that he had been drunk at the Rousseau banquet. He was just putting on an act to contribute to the fun, he explained. Matisse accused the author of neglecting Mrs. Michael Stein, whom he described as "the really intelligently sensitive member of the family." Matisse understandably was piqued because Gertrude Stein had said Madame Matisse had "a firm large loosely hung mouth like a horse." Jolas pompously dismissed the *Autobiography* for its "hollow tinsel bohemianism and egocentric deformations."

Some publishers say they'd rather have critics find fault with their books than ignore them. Maybe Gertrude Stein held a similar view. It was better to have old friends gang up on her than pay no attention at all. At any rate the attacks did not disturb her. They were, on the whole, petty and irrelevant. She had indeed done her associates a favor. She mentioned them in the one book above all that best described the creative climate of a historic time and place. She was certainly innocent of the animus they revealed. She held no brief against them, she wanted only to celebrate her own successes. Without the Jolases' instigation the "Testimony Against Gertrude Stein" would not have been compiled. There was even some question, as Gertrude Stein later implied, whether Braque had actually written the paragraphs attributed to him.

Gertrude Stein had tried repeatedly to persuade Ellery Sedgwick, editor of *The Atlantic Monthly,* to print something of hers. Of all American magazines she most longed to appear in that one. That was partly because it printed her dear friend Mildred Aldrich, now remembered for her wartime book, *Hilltop on the Marne.* Unhappily she got off on the wrong foot. She thought from a look at Sedgwick's signature that his name was not Ellery but Ellen. Consequently she addressed him as "Dear Miss Sedgwick." He corrected her amiably . . . but this is not recommended as a gambit for authors hoping to break into print. And he did keep saying no to her submissions. This changed to an enthusiastic yes when he received the manuscript of *The Autobiography of Alice B. Toklas.* The magazine published four installments.

Even the book's deliberate omissions reflected the nature of life in that faraway, long-ago Paris. You will not find the first name of the brother whose place Miss Toklas had usurped. You will not find the name of the man who, over Gertrude Stein's objections, got more space in *transition* than she did: James Joyce. Yet this is the essence of Left Bank life: rivalry, pettiness, grandeur, fits of spite, and most of all the healthy, frenzied, hard-working time that it really was.

Gertrude Stein was unabashedly inaccurate. Her letters to the Kiddie were addressed sometimes to W. K. Rogers and sometimes to Rodgers. She put an unneeded *c* in Braque and made it Bracque. She spelled Nathalie instead of Natalie Barney. Occasionally she dropped the dieresis on the *y* in Bernard Faÿ. She could spell Virgil Thomson Thompson. She left out the second *r* in Miguel Covarrubias. She was aware she could slip up on details. It didn't matter. She didn't bother to check. Always she must hurry on. Yet she did sometimes skirt tidily around a problem. For instance there was Sacheverell Sitwell. Everyone knew there were also Edith Sitwell and Osbert Sitwell. So it must be plain whom she meant if she ducked the touchy spelling challenge and put him in her script as S. Sitwell.

Was she wrong when she referred to herself as a genius? That must be considered in a certain context. Leo Stein in *Appreciations: Painting, Poetry and Prose* defines genius as "simply creativity." He added that "its opposite is routine." In that sense there is a vast amount of genius around. He even had a streak of it himself. Gertrude was demonstrably one hundred and ten percent genius. So calling herself a genius wasn't egotism, it was merely perfunctory pigeon-holing.

148

16 *I am solemnly going on writing the lectures.*

—LETTER TO THE KIDDIE

Gertrude Stein had found it good for her writing to live in France. "It was not what France gave you but what it did not take away from you that was important," she explained. The language she heard around her did not interfere with the language in which she wrote. It kept her thoughts completely within an unadulterated English. Her French, in fact, was rudimentary. The haphazard lessons from Fernande Olivier had not been much help to Miss Toklas, either. Gertrude Stein's accent was flagrantly American. No one has explained how she managed the faultless French of the two or three books she professedly wrote in that language. In *Everybody's Autobiography* she said, "I talk French badly and I write it worse." To the Kiddie she admitted that writing in French was hard. It could well have been impossible. Somebody helped but we don't know who.

"I am an American and I have lived half my life in Paris, not the half that made me but the half in which I made what I made," she reported. She had thought, though not seriously, of going back to the States. Friends and acquaintances now began to suggest she should return. In 1934 a major New York lecture bureau offered a contract for a countrywide tour. In one way it was a flattering proposition. In another way it was not. It seemed to Gertrude Stein and the practical Miss Toklas that the bureau's fee would be the lion's share of the proceeds. Yet Gertrude Stein was the lion-to-be. A Paris friend, William Aspenwall Bradley, wanted to give the project a try. He had already served as her literary agent and placed the Toklas *Autobiography* with its American publisher.

The two women studied the idea exhaustively. The talks at Oxford and Cambridge had been a success. Though Gertrude Stein had not made much money on them, she had made friends. She had enjoyed the confrontations. Her name was known in the States thanks to the Toklas book and the performance of *Four Saints in Three Acts* in the two cities: Hartford and New York . . . Chicago came later. What Gertrude Stein and Miss Toklas could not have realized at that moment was that the times were propitious. World War I had ended fifteen years before, but new calamities were brewing. Mussolini and Hitler were pushing arrogantly into the limelight. Verbal criticism of the Versailles peace treaty was developing ominously into action. The United States was fighting a serious depression. The dispirited public would welcome some relief, some headlines that were not all scare and gloom. This sibylline woman from Paris might be the answer to the need for something fresh, positive and heartening.

But there was another side to it. Add together the people who knew about her and the total was probably more foes than friends. The man in the street didn't understand her. What was worse, he laughed. She was friends with strange artists like Picasso, whose painting was to many as incomprehensible as her writing. Picabia, Matisse, Gris, Appollinaire were the odd-sounding names of her friends. By conventional female standards she was no beauty, and even that could not fairly be said of her devoted companion. She dressed outlandishly . . . as did Miss Toklas. Was there something queer about the two women living together all these years? Gertrude Stein was a Jew. There was a lot more anti-Semitism then than now and Jewish writers were rarer. Her own family had to an extent repudiated her; might not the public do likewise? Until the early 1930's her work had been read by a distressingly small public. Would her lecture audience be any bigger? Would she perhaps fill one medium-sized hall once . . . and no more? Edith Sitwell had argued that personal appearances helped with "half-intelligent people." If she had been proved right in England, would she now be proved wrong?

Gertrude Stein discussed the problem with her longtime friend and adviser Carl Van Vechten. Once a critic on *The New York Times*, and a novelist with a considerable readership, he had now abandoned the typewriter for the camera. He was beginning a huge collection of film portraits of leaders in all cultural fields. Many of them were Negroes. The Hartford *Four Saints* had struck him as pure delight. He strongly urged Gertrude Stein to make the tour.

At that time the Kiddie visited Bilignin. The women talked about the proposed trip. What did the Kiddie think? He said by all means come. He was on vacation from his newspaper. Back on the job, he began to have second thoughts. How did his managing editor estimate her chances? He was not sure. Both of them newsmen, they should have been dependable judges of her newsworthiness. There was no doubt that she would attract the most lively attention from a small group. But would she interest the masses? Allowing for his prejudice, the Kiddie still thought it was worth the risk.

Gertrude Stein went to work on a set of six lectures. She also decided against engaging Bradley as agent. As she wrote the Kiddie, "We could not see eye to eye in this matter, I to I if you like." Instead, she enlisted the services of a young art scholar at the moment jobless . . . like many others in those depression years. He was to operate in close association with Miss Toklas. There was one stipulation: Gertrude Stein would not address an audience of more than five hundred. The Kiddie meanly suspected she laid down this rule with her tongue in her cheek. To specify that the audience must not be too large was a way of reassuring herself. It amounted to the assumption that it would not be too small.

The association with the young American did not pan out. Miss Toklas on her own took over the task of arranging dates and setting fees. She hoped the Kiddie would be able to help? He would gladly do all he could. He was living in Springfield, Massachusetts. It was a conservative region even though *Four Saints* had premiered not far away. If colleges or clubs in that area could be interested, that should augur well for Gertrude Stein's reception elsewhere. The Kiddie was not an able agent and he wasn't merely lucky. He happened to have a top-notch, A-Number One product to sell. Three organizations in Springfield snapped her up at once and signed on the dotted line. The Kiddie's college, Amherst, a few miles up the Connecticut Valley, took her on. So did Mount Holyoke, Wesleyan, the Connecticut College for Women, the city of Hartford, the Pittsfield art museum. She was booked solid for more than two weeks in that neck of the woods.

Back in Bilignin the women began to get ready in earnest. First of all they needed clothes. Longtime Parisiennes, they might have been expected to rely on the famous *couturières* of their home city. On the contrary they were sure that dressmakers in Belley or some other nearby town could fit them satisfactorily. Miss Toklas had a weakness for pins, bracelets and necklaces. That was, incidentally, something of a fashion; Edith Sitwell wore rings as long as her finger and other eye-catching jewelry. Gertrude Stein liked adornment that was not ornamental. They would wear what they had always worn. If they didn't make the fashion, at least fashion didn't make them. They very much wanted to dress well but according to their ideas and not someone else's. One invariable characteristic of their clothing was that it must be heavy. They were used to underheated French interiors.

Gertrude Stein wrote to the Kiddie, "I am solemnly going on writing the lectures. I have finished one about pictures, one about the theatre, and am now doing the one about English literature. Then there are three about my work, Making of Americans, 2 Portraits and so-called repetition and what is and what is not, 3 Grammar and tenses." She did not italicize the title of her novel. The two numerals, 2 and 3, mean the second and third subjects. It was a wide field to be covered by a woman who years before had specifically renounced all knowledge as her province. She mailed the Kiddie the lectures. He dutifully and accurately pronounced them wonderful. They were published as *Lectures in America* the following year.

Then she wanted to know about food. She was sixty years old and must be careful about her diet. She was used to French food, the best but also the simplest. She hoped there would not be a drastic change. The Kiddie sent her a representative selection of hotel menus. She and Miss Toklas had a theory that French food was drier. For that reason the French drank wine with their meals. American food, on the other hand, was supposedly more moist. This in part compensated for the drier air in our overheated rooms.

Miss Toklas deserves all the credit for the superlative meals served at the rue de Fleurus and at Bilignin. She used to do the marketing. Early in the morning she took her string bag and set out by trolley or bus for the old Halles Centrales. In those days it was the marketplace for all Paris. Miss Toklas' eye for food was even sharper than her eye for geniuses. If no bell rang, something within her clicked at the freshest, and only the freshest, tastiest, tenderest vegetables. The cut of meat must be absolutely right . . . right color, resiliency, smell, proportion of fat to lean.

You had only to watch her select a roast of lamb. She asked everything about it except the animal's pedigree. She told the butcher what to cut off, where to cut, what to leave on, how to wrap it round and round with a web of string. She knew as much about meat as he did. It's hard to imagine what she would do today if she were obliged to rummage around in a supermarket counter of packaged meat. Such a painstaking customer might have offended an American clerk. The French butcher, on the contrary, recognized a master. He welcomed someone so knowledgeable. Her very presence proved his shop offered the best meats.

Neither woman was heard to complain about American food once it became their daily fare. But in view of their fabulous reception in their native land, any complaint about anything would have been incredible.

17 *I always did like to be a lion.*

—EVERYBODY'S AUTOBIOGRAPHY

Gertrude Stein and Miss Toklas sailed from Le Havre on the French Line's *Champlain.* Celebrities, we may suppose, benefit from a courtesy reduction in fare. They reached New York on October 24, 1934. In those days, and perhaps now, though there are fewer passenger liners, a Coast Guard cutter met ships down the bay by the Statue of Liberty. It carried customs and medical officers, who could thus start their checks early and finish them by docking time. Reporters seeking interviews got a ride.

The Kiddie went along. The little boat was loaded. One reason for the crowd could be the *abbé* Ernest Dimnet, a popular French philosopher and lecturer. Were the newsmen hoping for stories from him? Were they going to question Gertrude Stein? Or were they gunning for her? Would they bring the projected tour to a rough, tough end there and then?

156

Gertrude Stein and Alice B. Toklas arrive in New York, October 24, 1934. (The Bettmann Archive.)

A top deck is a dizzy distance above the waterline. But as the cutter drew alongside, the Kiddie looked up and saw his two friends leaning over the rail. He waved, they waved. It was a long climb up to them. A small public room had been prepared and there the old friends met and exchanged hugs. A table was set up. Radio and newsreel teams were laying heavy, snakelike electric cables around for the unwary to trip over. Practically the whole flock of newsmen made for Gertrude Stein.

She sat apparently calm at the table. The inquisitors drew out their pencils like daggers from scabbards and readied their notebooks. The battle royal was joined. It seemed obvious to the Kiddie that the reporters had come in a doubting, cynical mood. This presumptuous lady might get away with it in Paris but not in sophisticated New York.

She won them all over in no time flat. She didn't make a single fumble. They fired the sort of questions she was used to after decades of parrying them. Why didn't she talk the way she wrote? She retorted, "Why don't you read the way I write?" She scored this telling point: "You reporters don't talk as you write." She was here, she said, "to tell very plainly and simply and directly, as is my fashion, what literature is." She cleverly ducked inquiries about politics. She identified Miss Toklas as her secretary. In a half hour she made a roomful not necessarily of friends but of converts and advocates.

Harsh experience had taught the Kiddie how a reporter can bring in a good story . . . he thinks it's good . . . only to have a city editor kill it. Most of it is red-penciled, only the first and last paragraphs survive. Or perhaps the whole story is chucked into the wastebasket. Here aboard ship it was clear that the reporters had dug out some vivid, colorful copy. They had encountered a genuine personality, an eccentric, and every one of them appreciated it. She also happened to be, according to rumor, a great writer. But what would the city editor do?

Evidently city editors didn't change a word. Four New York papers—there were lots of papers in those halcyon years—featured the Stein story on page one. There were generous spreads of Gertrude Stein's round, sculptural face, friendly, unmystifying, contented. The headlines, it is true, mocked her style:

GERTY GERTY STEIN STEIN
IS BACK HOME HOME BACK

Even so the heavy black type stretched several columns wide. She had met the true enemy, the hard-shell reporter, and he was hers.

The encounter with the press over, the pictures all taken, customs procedures complied with, she went ashore. Bennett Cerf, her current publisher, and Carl Van Vechten drove her to the Algonquin Hotel. There the newcomers settled in a suite. They granted further interviews to admiring newsmen. In an evening walk around the block, passersby already recognized the author. She was particularly impressed when a man blurted out to his woman companion, "There goes your friend Gertrude Stein." The five-and-tens disappointed her. She loved the nut stores. In Times Square she had only to look up to see her name in huge electric lights. It was flashed on the illuminated news band that ran around the *New York Times* building then standing in that space.

It's hard to realize what recognition on this unprecedented scale meant. For almost half a century this woman had had to fight for a hearing. Countless rebuffs rocked her back on her heels. She had worked and worked and earned precious little at her chosen calling. And now victory, triumph! Heroine in her native land! She loved it. She quoted Alfred Stieglitz's comment on her spectacular successes: "It is just a Christmas tree for you all the time." She added, "which it is." The huzzas rang out and the red carpet rolled out before she delivered even one lecture.

The Kiddie heard twelve or fifteen lectures, most of them in New England. The first was of course the crucial one. For this the Colony Club in New York was the host. That was a week after she landed. "I did have stage fright," she confessed. It was a waste of her nervous energy. Everything went extremely well. In all the audiences in the Kiddie's personal experience, only one discordant note sounded: a man let out an incredulous guffaw at some remark of hers. But lots of listeners probed sharply after her reading was finished. Some of them went at her hammer and tongs. Shouldn't writing make sense? Shouldn't one abide by the rules of grammar? What was the point of saying the same thing over and over? It cannot be pretended that her answers invariably satisfied the doubters. But she made them take her seriously. The fact that they couldn't understand, they began uneasily to suspect, might be their fault instead of hers. She was not a fraud, not a freak, not a literary sideshow. She was obviously informed about art and about writing. She was staking out a claim to a place in American literature. On the publication of the Toklas *Autobiography* some of columnist Henry McBride's readers had asked him if it was a spoof. There wasn't really any Gertrude Stein, was there? Now they knew. She had registered indelibly.

At once it was clear, too, that her restriction on the size of an audience was justifiable. At Columbia University a thousand and more persons turned up expecting to hear her. The number was cut ruthlessly.

She was royally entertained. She attended a football game at Yale. Van Vechten threw a big reception for her. Her publisher gave a party. She was the guest of New York's exclusive Dutch Treat Club. She even saw a performance of her opera, *Four Saints in Three Acts*. It was presented in Chicago. Her schedule called for her to lecture there but that was later. For this first trip she had her first plane ride. She enjoyed the singers immensely and was happy to meet them all. They were happy to meet her, too. They liked the words and understood them, they assured her, and they sang them with gusto.

She had a curious comment about *Four Saints*. She told Florine Stettheimer, the designer, she was glad the opera "was not the way I do not like it." That was very different from saying it was the way she did like it. The circumlocutions that were, in her mind, literature also had their practical uses. You couldn't take offense at this judgment, you couldn't point to it with pride, either. It was a subtle straddle. She didn't exactly say what she meant. She didn't exactly mean what she said. It left you up in the air. This mystification may have been a consequence of her disagreement, whatever it was, with the composer. Or it may have been another manifestation of her "bottom nature." She was niggardly with outright praise of any possible rival in the race for glory.

"I do want to get rich but I never want to do what there is to do to get rich," she had said. She might have put herself out to make friends, meet admirers halfway and comply with society's demands. It is just these demands that make the lecture circuit unendurable for some sensitive souls. Gertrude Stein on tour was on the whole unsociable. Perhaps Miss Toklas was the one to say no to the innumerable invitations to dinners, lunches, teas, parties, get-togethers of all sorts. Or perhaps Gertrude Stein herself made the decisions. She was here to lecture, not to be sociable. As between making friends and influencing people her exclusive aim was to influence people. This standoffishness may contrarily have made her presence all the more desirable. She was astute enough to appreciate that. Perhaps she did it for the simple reason that she had to husband her strength and energy. You would have expected Hartford, which launched *Four Saints,* to be able to command her presence. She said no to all Hartford overtures. The best she did was to attend a tea in the suburb of Farmington. She was not in the States to show gratitude to anyone for anything. Mabel Dodge, staunch proselytizer of years before, asked to be received and was turned down.

In Pittsfield the museum director properly hoped that Gertrude Stein would attend a small, select reception. The

162

reply was no. She was disconcertingly frank in her refusals, too. One hostess proffered some elegant refreshments. No thanks, said the distinguished visitor, but she would like a nice red apple. The red-faced hostess didn't have an apple in the house. None of this was personal. The calendar must be kept clear for the business at hand. Gertrude Stein did not bear grudges . . . though Miss Toklas did. As Miss Toklas said of herself and of a friend: one forgot but did not forgive, the other forgave but did not forget. With one excuse or another, Gertrude Stein and Miss Toklas kept the celebrity hunters at bay.

In Springfield the two expatriates had the leisure to relax. The Kiddies served them a few lunches. A friend of ours took them for a sleigh ride. They saw the trim, well ordered, immemorial New England countryside. The French countryside was neat, too, but neat in a practical and efficient way. New England was neat out of pride and habit, and it impressed Gertrude Stein. She visited Deerfield Academy and the town of Deerfield, scene of an Indian massacre more than two centuries earlier.

She stopped in a local bookstore and autographed copies of her works. Stein autographs were strewn all over the land. She was never at a loss for a phrase to scribble on a flyleaf. The Kiddie once visited with her the country home of Jean-Jacques Rousseau, the eighteenth-century romantic philosopher. There was a guest book. She rattled off something in a flash and at the bottom dashed off the usual abbreviated signature, "Gtde Stein." This sort of chore took the Kiddie minutes. Her autographs were collected in a pamphlet, "Chicago Inscriptions." One was in *Four*

Saints for the critic Fanny Butcher: "Dear fanny you are the best of famous Fans and Famous, but the best the very best of Fannies, and always my affection Gtde." There are a lot of them in the Kiddie's books. In *The Making of Americans* she wrote, "For Mildred and for the Kiddies, Yes yes a thousand times yes For a nice Mildred and for a nice Kiddie, yes oh yes a thousand times yes oh yes Gtde."

"A thousand times yes" was a phrase picked up here from an advertisement. Some happenings, too, got into her books. At a lunch in the Kiddies' apartment a dish was burned to a smoking crisp in the antiquated gas oven. In all the excitement of having these two famous friends at our table, the stern husband reminded Mrs. Kiddie about the balky stove: "Let this be a lesson to you." So Gertrude Stein heard about it and spread the admonition here and there through later pages. During the first early visit at Mabel Dodge's in Italy something had been stolen. The first houseman was presumed to be innocent but not the second. Hence the frequent phrase, "Suspect the second man."

On an auto trip to Providence, Rhode Island, we sang songs to while away the time. Among them was Gertrude Stein's favorite, "On the Trail of the Lonesome Pine." We sang the wartime "Madelon" and "Sur le Pont d'Avignon." Mrs. Kiddie contributed a popular radio ditty which advertised a bakery product: "Yo ho yo ho yo ho yo ho for we are the makers of Wonder Bread." That song got into subsequent Stein prose, too. A famous group of American painters was known as the Ashcan School. It got its name because these artists put the commonplace, the ordinary, the back-alley scenes on their canvases. Gertrude Stein was doing the same thing. She used the commonplace, the trivial, the everyday.

The two travelers went all the way west to San Francisco. In Hollywood they met Charlie Chaplin, star of silent films, and Dashiell Hammett, author of crisp, realistic mystery stories much admired by Gertrude Stein. How did you get to be so famous? the stars of the screen asked enviously. Her answer surprised them. They wanted to be seen by millions and millions of moviegoers. She said she made her name "by having a small audience."

In Chicago her meeting with Thornton Wilder began one of her most rewarding friendships. Chicago police in a patrol car showed her the city's seamier side. She went back later for still another visit to lecture at the University of Chicago.

At the Choate School in Connecticut the youngsters almost mobbed her with their persistent questioning. Several boys who made her acquaintance during those frenzied months have since said they had taken it for granted she was a phony until seeing and hearing her changed their minds.

One tangible aspect of the lecture tour was that it was profitable. Gertrude Stein wrote the Kiddie, with more feeling than she usually cared to show, how wonderful it was to have some extra money. For years the two women had got along but not much more than got along. They had had servants, they had eaten well, they had traveled on the Continent. On their income, however, they could hardly have lived so well in the United States. Europe was then, as it has always been until recent years, much cheaper than America. Spain and Italy were less expensive than France. To be sure, Gertrude Stein made some judicious art sales. A canvas bought for a song was occasionally sold for several thousand dollars. But such transactions were rare. She bought pictures not as an investment but because she loved them. Just before her death she was paid five hundred dollars for the libretto of *The Mother of Us All*, her second opera to be produced. *Four Saints* bolstered her exchequer. The Toklas *Autobiography* helped more. The tour helped most of all. *Everybody's Autobiography* reports excitedly about "the sudden splendid spending of money."

It was at last time to ring down the curtain. The return to France was booked on the *Champlain*. The tour had been a phenomenal, an incomparable success. Was the Latin poet Virgil crowned by his grateful emperor? Are novelists knighted in England? Did hundreds of thousands march at the funeral of Victor Hugo? All this seems little compared to the apotheosis of Gertrude Stein on this trip. It was all the more remarkable because writers are of necessity lone wolves. They are obliged to be separated from their audience. Actors are cheered, musicians are applauded. Writers betake themselves to the garret, shut the door and work in miserable loneliness and isolation. Millions may read them, only handfuls ever see them. Gertrude Stein was a signal exception. The trumpets sounded, the walls came tumbling down, and lo, the writer! She could have wept at this triumph.

Just before they left, Miss Toklas wrote the Kiddie about

"the marvellous-marvellous-marvellous visit" . . . the double *l* in "marvellous" is British so this can't properly qualify as a misspelling. And this was no repetition for literary effect. It came straight from the heart. Gertrude Stein felt the same way only more so. According to a letter of hers:

> Everything . . . was wonderful we were awfully moved, for it was wonderful and we knew it was wonderful every minute it was being wonderful and I did not really realize it was over until I suddenly said to Alice but now I have got to be putting U. S. A. on the envelope and then I had a kind of shock of really knowing that it was really over.

Back in Paris, in an interview with a newsman, she said, "Yes, I am married." This surprise was enough to bowl him over. Then she added, "I mean I am married to America."

18 *Remarks are not literature.*
—THE AUTOBIOGRAPHY OF ALICE B. TOKLAS

Some things cannot be said clearly and definitively. They are only felt. A flood of tears, a burst of laughter, a Beethoven symphony, a Picasso collage often defy translation into the ordinary, utilitarian vocabulary. The words used to pass the time of day, gossip over the card table or order groceries cannot be depended on to interpret a musical composition or a painting. We can come near but a gap remains. Gertrude Stein's ideas partake of this elusive nature. You sense them. You divine them by a sort of extrasensory perception, you absorb or inhale them. They are like a mountain peak glimpsed through autumn fog. Such ideas are valid . . . the peak is there. But they are hard or impossible to put your finger on. Someone said we should try to read Gertrude Stein as she tried to write. That's fair enough. Consider this sentence from *How to Write*, published in 1931:

> If it does not decide beside will it be a formal hope that this is that when there are they will call by it in a delay coming as a call which is belied which is it after the and blessing as in noon which can always be cordially a name left alone with invited as they return and gone as farther without relief of as much made in a wait waiting about which is where after is amount amount to it likewise rested made an opposition to sewn it was very well sewn because they will allow for tapestry.

At once Gertrude Stein added, as if to beat the baffled reader to it, "now this is a difficult sentence." That is not literally true, for it is not difficult. Different, yes; difficult, no. If you take it as you take the sentences you were brought up with, sentences learned in grammar school, it is a stickler. It is difficult if you expect the conventional succession of words. By now, of course, you should not expect the normal. You read Gertrude Stein for the reason that she does lead you merrily away from the beaten path. She does that here. She often handled words one at a time, not in a group or flock. There is no crowd, no mass. There is always the separate, individual existence. That's the story of this sentence. The words do not join hands. They simply march along Indian file. It is one and one and one and one.

This word conglomeration is proof of a fantastic ingenuity. It is about as hard to lead without sense from one word to another as to lead sensibly. Perhaps it's harder . . . you might try. Out of what depths of her trailblazing mind did she dig up this particular verbal succession? What inimitable quirks in her brain cells led her from connectives that do not connect to verbs that do not act to nouns that do not take the place of persons or things? A sentence, she warned, is not emotional. A paragraph is. A sentence, she meant, has a fixed and inviolable form. You can't monkey with it. A paragraph bends at your will. It permits variety. In that sense the passage just quoted resembles a paragraph rather than a sentence. It is as long as a paragraph, too. This "difficult" sentence is a sort of grab bag, a button box of a vocabulary. Dip in and come up with a plum. Like other Stein sentences, it starts off here, veers over there, turns back on itself, somersaults and heads somewhere else. I follow it religiously.

She did not set out to hoodwink the reading world. It was no hoax. She meant with her whole head and heart everything she was doing. There was only one kind of criticism that the Kiddie resented. It was the charge that she was not in earnest. Writers are fair game. They stick their necks out. The worst marksmen as well as the best take aim and fire again and again. But there was never any justification for accusing Gertrude Stein of being a cheat. Of the many rebuttals, the most effective is the most obvious. Nobody goes in for a lifetime of cheating. Dishonesty wears itself out. Besides, if cheating it was, it clearly was getting her nowhere during the first ten years or the second ten or even the third. Long before then she would have quit. People at Harvard and Johns Hopkins stated publicly that she had brains. Having brains means that she would have seen she was accomplishing nothing. To say that she was a fraud, then, is to say also that she was a numbskull. She was not.

She was not only a creative writer but also a theorist about writing. You may sometimes think she just blindly creates. On the contrary, she herself knew what she was doing. She discussed her aims and methods in *How to Write, The Geographical History of America, What Are Masterpieces, Lectures in America* and other books. She and her works have been studied exhaustively in half a dozen books of commentary and in the learned introductions to her eight posthumous volumes. One of the most understanding and sympathetic readers has been Thornton Wilder. She was a metaphysician, he thought, and an artist who was often gay as serious artists often are not. She was "an impassioned listener to life," as he saw her. He regarded her work as a "series of spiritual exercises."

"Write" and "right" in her view are not necessarily connected. This leads to her distinction between human nature and the human mind. Human nature is the lesser and weaker. Human nature writes with the aim of addressing an audience. It does not exist for itself alone, it is practical, it intends to leave its mark. Human mind is purer. It is abstract like modern painting. It is dissociated from what has the appearance of the real.

What counted for Gertrude Stein the writer was spontaneity. Radio and TV give us what are promoted as unrehearsed programs. Her writing was truly unrehearsed, it was "live." This, too, was the province of the human mind

171

and beyond the area proper to human nature. Novelists correct, rewrite, emend, add and subtract. University libraries collect tons of manuscripts covered with arrows, interlinear notations, additions, erasures. They are all by the kind of writer Gertrude Stein definitely was not. She just wrote and wrote and wrote and that was it. The novel, essay, or poem sprang full-blown from her august brow. No slightest change was conceivable. Hands off!

If it came out pristine and unadulterated from the human mind, it was of necessity original. Copying, she said, doesn't amount to anything. It accomplishes nothing. It gives the copier no feeling of excitement. All that matters is doing something never done before . . . countless Stein contemporaries in the creative fields would agree with this. This brand-new thing . . . poem, painting, essay, novel . . . invariably has something ugly in it. That explains, she said, why it takes so long for the exploratory and experimental to win acceptance. She brings her point home dramatically with a compelling argument. To appreciate Raphael, she said, we must look and look at his paintings until we see again what was originally ugly in them. Over the centuries the public has come to label some of his work not merely beautiful but cloyingly beautiful, even sentimental. Hunt for the ugly beyond all that to get at the true Raphael.

"Remarks are not literature," she warned the neophyte Ernest Hemingway. She didn't specifically mean aphorisms or adages. Her ban applied to informational statements. Yet the remark itself falls within the area of her general condemnation. In this respect Hemingway is not abundantly quotable. Gertrude Stein, on the contrary, is. Many people remember her not as the author of operas, plays and novels but for her own "remarks." She characterized Hemingway and his contemporaries as the "lost generation." The phrase has become ingrained in the literary vernacular. "Rose is a rose is a rose is a rose," "pigeons on the grass alas," "Toasted susie is my ice-cream" are widely familiar. Some of her phrases are firmly established in the traditional collections of memorable quotations.

Yet Gertrude Stein was right. Isolated remarks do not make literature. Literature is more than "bits of information and tender feeling," as she said. It is unjust to remember only the oddities, however brilliant. She deserves to be read in bulk. I do not mean she should be read *in toto*. Some Stein is better than other Stein. No one should try to "take" all Stein all at once . . . or all Shakespeare either, for that matter. But she has a right to be heard. She is rewarding in *Tender Buttons, Four Saints, Three Lives* and other works as wholes or units. The reader must follow the advice of William James: Be open-minded.

She complained that newspapers fail in their chief purpose. They do not make news sound up-to-the-minute. She believed there is a time lag. The question of time ranked in importance in her day with the question of consciousness. They were indeed associated. She could have learned about time as the fourth dimension from Henri Bergson, her contemporary in Paris. What she tried to capture, or represent, or create, was the continuous present, the going on and going on and going on. She strived for immediacy. There used to be a popular Edward R. Murrow radio program, "You Are There." That is where Gertrude Stein tried to place you as she wrote.

We are inclined to suppose she created in a vacuum. Nobody does really. There are always ties to something in the past and in the present. There are links, above all, to the vague, indefinable but very real spirit of the times. Some of Gertrude Stein's idiosyncrasies were family idiosyncrasies. She was influenced by her brother Leo, by Picasso, by William James, by the air she and they, too, all breathed. The Greeks owe their genius in part to their land, the rocky promontory that juts down magnificently into the Mediterranean. The Americans were formed in part by the laborious, bold acquisition of a vast continent, by the conquest of the West. America got under Gertrude Stein's skin. Flying over her country she saw patterns in fields and forests resembling the patterns in Picasso paintings. They were patterns that he, in turn, had brought back from his native Spain. The motherland is a far spreading, inclusive web. Gertrude Stein both broke away and stayed put. There was something exclusively, uniquely Gertrude Stein, something inherited, something borrowed, something absorbed and blotted up at home and abroad.

Gertrude Stein and Miss Toklas lived together almost forty years. One reflected the other. In their thinking it was hard to tell where one began and the other left off. They dressed alike, behaved alike and to a degree thought and talked alike. That was inevitable. They knew the same people, had the same experiences. Miss Toklas was as anxious to get Gertrude Stein published as Gertrude Stein was herself. The two streams joined in one river . . . though the Stein current ran broader and deeper.

Perhaps the most consequential link was with Leo. Gertrude Stein had been his companion thirty or more years. Miss Toklas occupied the rue de Fleurus home four years before he left it. His imprint remained: banished, the ghost was still there. One passage in Leo's *Appreciation: Painting, Poetry and Prose*, could have been written by his sister. She wrote badly, he charged, because she didn't know any better. As he meant the adverb "badly," this passage below is also bad writing. It supposedly reproduces someone else's speech. Matisse's teacher had commented on his work. Leo quoted Matisse's own version of what the teacher had said. It just proves that a Stein is a Stein is a Stein:

> Well, you know, of course not everybody sees things as everybody else does, and of course one can't judge fairly when one is not sure just how someone else sees things who sees them differently from the way one sees them, and in that case one might say the wrong thing if one said anything, since one isn't sure where the other person stands in relation to oneself.

It has more commas than Gertrude Stein would have used. Otherwise what is this but a continuous present, her repetitions, her talking-around a subject as a method for boxing it in? If she had written this, Leo would have been sure to complain of "bad" writing. A lot of writers at first seem obscure to their contemporaries. This obscurity, this difficulty inherent in the new, is an aspect of the ugliness Gertrude Stein urged us to rediscover in Raphael. Occasional sentences in William Faulkner require reading twice. Browning Clubs used to labor over glosses of passages in Robert Browning's *The Ring and the Book*. Will there be Stein clubs to explicate some of her difficult prose?

But as we remember parts of Browning, say, and not other parts, so time will weed out the lasting works of Gertrude Stein. We should stop grouching about what isn't good and start crediting what is. More than one critic has quoted admiringly Sherwood Anderson's praise of her "little housekeeping words, the swaggering bullying street-corner words, the honest working money saving words." She fired them with a fresh life and vitality.

19   *. . . to send melons two melons to them, this*
     makes them give to you their blessing.

—PORTRAITS AND PRAYERS

Two years after Gertrude Stein and Miss Toklas went back to France, the Kiddies followed them there for a visit to Bilignin. It was 1937. The Paris World's Fair, the *Exposition Mondiale,* was spectacularly housed along the Seine opposite the Eiffel Tower. In Spain Generalissimo Francisco Franco was leading a bloody revolt against the people's government. The warplanes of his allies the Germans had destroyed the town of Guernica. A highlight of the Paris show commemorated that ghastly raid. It was the great mural *Guernica,* by Gertrude Stein's Spanish-born friend Picasso, exhibited in the Spanish Pavilion.

Gertrude Stein had Thornton Wilder with her when she met the Kiddies at the railway junction of Virieu. We settled in at the Stein-Toklas summer home. That evening there was a barn dance in a nearby village. An accordion

177

The sitting room at Bilignin as seen by an English friend, the artist Francis Rose, in 1938.

and a fiddle furnished the music. They were perhaps a little off tune and a little ragged but very lively. Thornton Wilder and the Kiddie danced with the local girls while the womenfolks looked on approvingly. It was not the smooth gliding movement we were used to. It was a hop-hop-hoppity step, like jogging. It was, anyway, welcome exercise after sitting for hours in a train. The next day we drove along Lake Geneva. Thornton Wilder left to go to Zurich. Gertrude Stein showed us the gray, waterbound

Castle of Chillon, romantically commemorated in Byron's "The Prisoner of Chillon." We returned just as the Alpine glow turned the snowy summit of Mont Blanc pink.

In the following days we paid calls on neighborhood friends. We walked over the grounds of the estate where the woman either "suicided herself," as the French say, or was murdered. We visited the sister of dramatist Paul Claudel. We had a gay dinner at the Château de Béon. This was the home of the Baroness Pierlot. One son was a colonel. One day he would go tranquilly about his business. The next he would be ordered off at a minute's notice to the Maginot Line as the bellicose Hitler made another threatening gesture. This happened again and again. It was the Nazi technique for keeping the French on edge. The other son was Count François d'Aiguy. Red-faced, volatile observer of the political scene, he contributed learned editorials to the local newspaper, the *Bugiste*. Later he sent the Kiddie clippings in the hope they could be published in the United States. The articles eventually appeared in book form. We window-shopped in Chambéry. We dined at the water's edge by Lake Annécy. We visited the Abbey of Hautecombe, burial place of Italy's royal House of Savoy. A popular woman novelist entertained us at an outdoor buffet in Aix-les-Bains.

This was a prelude to a trip back to southern France, where the Kiddie's friendship with Gertrude Stein had begun. Gertrude Stein had written before we sailed:

> Do you know what we are going to do we are going to drive ourselves to Avignon Arles St. Remy Les Baux and then sleep at Nimes and go to Uzes and St. Gilles

and Aiguesmortes and Vienne and back to Bilignin and all the way Mrs. Kiddy will listen to the remembering of all of us and the very best time will be had by all, and Mrs. Kiddy instead of singing Wonder Bread will sing Nougat Nougat as we go in and out of Montelimar, and as soon as you make up your mind let us know that you are coming, won't it be wonderful to do all that together again. . . .

The letter was shy on question marks, accents, commas and so on. She wrote "Kiddy," though it was usually spelled "Kiddie." But the trip would certainly all be most wonderful.

Greatness or genius is often flawed by personal crotchets that are hard to put up with. It isn't really domesticated. We'd like to have dinner or spend an evening with some novelists or poets but we wouldn't like to live with them. But Gertrude Stein and Miss Toklas together day in and day out were warmhearted hostesses. They were thoughtful, attentive, full of fun, always bubbling over with good talk. In the Kiddies' experience their social or literary preeminence never interfered with their roles as friends. Gertrude Stein loved to talk about writing, especially her own writing . . . and who wouldn't have loved to hear her? While the Kiddies were there, she gave them the manuscript of *Mrs. Reynolds* to read and, naturally, enjoy. As Gertrude Stein's United States trip had been one long Christmas tree, so was the Kiddies' Bilignin visit. It was a tree and trimmings and the lights all twinkling.

The dog Basket was a *caniche royale*, or royal poodle. He was slightly spoiled. What's the point of having a dog unless you spoil him a little? Too big to go on the trip, he was left with a nearby veterinarian. Miss Toklas' kitten-sized Chihuahua, Pepe, though he was almost too little, was nevertheless to keep us company.

Miss Toklas was the practical partner. She believed in schedules, plans, itineraries. Gertrude Stein wanted nothing to do with such precision and exactitude. She disliked being tied down. She preferred spur-of-the-minute decisions. She let nature take its course. It was her habit, for instance, to get up when she waked. She would not tolerate an alarm clock. When daylight came, when she was rested, her eyes just naturally opened. She would then look through the morning paper. At last, leisurely, she got up. She went into the bathroom, threw open the heavy wood shutters and gazed out on the morning. I think she particularly relished appearing in that framework. She surveyed a wide land falling away before her. She was the lord and master of all she saw, and more, too. Cut off by the high sill, seen from the waist up, she was a squarish figure. The tall oblong window opening stretched up above her. She was outlined sharply against the dark interior. She called down cheerily to guests on the terrace. They were eating Miss Toklas' delectable breakfast served on trays. Gertrude Stein would join them when she got good and ready and not a minute before.

Anyone planning a long trip would much prefer the methodical ways of Miss Toklas. She proposed starting at nine o'clock. She proposed it a few days before we left. She mentioned it several times. It was sort of like talking to herself. But Gertrude Stein did hear her and at last remarked that nine was a fine hour. She would be ready, she said pacifyingly, when everyone was ready. Miss Toklas was doubtful. She compromised. Let's start early, she suggested, not so positively yet not quite meekly, either. Early was fine, too, Gertrude Stein agreed, pacing up and down calmly with her fingers tucked in the shallow pockets of her skirt.

Actually we got off at ten-thirty. We were lucky to do as well as that. The rest of us, long since packed, had been loitering by the door a half-hour or so. Then Gertrude Stein marched out of the house. She climbed hastily into the driver's seat before we could reach the car. She got even with Miss Toklas:

"Here I am and where is everyone else?"

The luggage was stowed away. There was a lot of it, too, including food for Pepe and a special dark bread for Gertrude Stein. Miss Toklas sat in back with Pepe in her lap. Mrs. Kiddie sat beside her. The Kiddie was beside the driver. The starter hummed. The motor roared. Madame Roux, the woman of all work, tugged at the big iron gate and swung it wide open. She squeezed back against it . . . wise woman, knowing who was about to try to steer a car close by her. She waved good-by. Gertrude Stein launched us with a jerk. We reached for leather like a cowboy on a bucking bronco. We flew safely out to the main road and were on our way.

We all knew Laurence Sterne's *Sentimental Journey Through France and Italy*. This was our "sentimental journey." Gertrude Stein always kept one hand on the wheel but rarely two. The thumb and forefinger of the idle hand incessantly pinched and tugged at a strand of her short gray hair. She kept an eye on the road except when she talked. For conversation she liked to turn and face the Kiddie squarely. There was a lot of conversation. But nothing untoward happened. Everything went smoothly, there wasn't even a near-miss. The worst mishap was a flat tire. In the end the Kiddie proved to be the negligent one. He changed the tire. When we got back to the States, a letter chided him. The hubcap on that wheel had fallen off, which means that he couldn't have pounded it back on securely.

It was market day when we drove through the little town of Romans. We stopped to admire the displays. Ripe figs, plums, pink and yellow pears, grapes and, prophetically, melons were spread out on trays on stands and on the ground. There were also kitchen utensils, hardware, wooden shoes, a little bit of everything. We eyed the townspeople: corduroys, aprons, kerchiefs. They eyed us: fat woman, thin woman, a pair of foreigners and a ridiculous little dog. Pepe had his first walk or, as it was called, doodle. The old weatherbeaten church had dark stone walls, narrow windows and a skimpy porch. Miss Toklas slipped in to leave an offering for Saint Anthony. He is the patron of those who, like Miss Toklas, lose things or mislay them. Then we drove on to Montélimar and loaded up with bars of nougat.

One of the Kiddie's functions was to read maps. The French didn't number their roads, or not the ones on which we traveled. Americans could follow Route 10 or 20 or 30 coast to coast or Canada to Mexico. The French depended on Michelin guides. They were, and are, excellent. But they can't be read at a glance. You have to pay close attention. To go through a town you wind around a church, pass a municipal hall and a cemetery, head through the main square and so on. Each of these is matched by a symbol on the detailed local map. Watch for the bend in the line on the map, watch for the steeple or whatever in the town itself. It is absolutely dependable but keep your mind on it. There are road signs, too. But Gertrude Stein had the habit of speeding right up to an intersection and through it. Then just beyond where the sign could be read she would cry in alarm, "Where do we go now? Tell me quickly! Kiddie!"

A plan to lunch in one town was abandoned when we were not able to find a suitable restaurant. The Kiddie missed a turning . . . or we by our joint fumbling missed it . . . and we found ourselves on a long bridge over the Rhône River. It was just where we did not want to go. Miss Toklas recommended an immediate about-face. Gertrude Stein, as was often the case, did not approve. Neither did the Kiddies. Ahead we caught intriguing glimpses of a town set high on a cliff, with red tile roofs and a church tower. It was Viviers, site of a Romanesque church and an old episcopal palace. One doesn't ask specifically for a good restaurant, our driver advised. One asks, "Where can we eat well?" A passing bicyclist gave us directions and he proved to be right. The only problem at table was Gertrude Stein. She secretly fed Pepe delicacies to which his stomach was not accustomed. Miss Toklas made her stop. After all, if the dog were to be

184

sick, he would be sick in Miss Toklas' lap. Gertrude Stein argued that the dog was hungry. He would be fed the proper food at the proper time and only that and only then, was the firm answer.

The next stop on our itinerary was Orange. We were now drawing close to our goal. The Kiddies wandered through the Roman theater. Miss Toklas stayed in the car. She liked a view but she liked to sit with her back to it. That was that she said and what she always did. Gertrude Stein poked around a market and came back with a big fresh ripe muskmelon. It probably weighed four pounds. In a hardware store the Kiddie bought a jackknife with one long blade. A little farther on we turned off the road to find a spot for a picnic. There were very few of the comfort stations available every mile or so along American highways. It was the French habit to stop right by the edge of the road whenever the need arose. The need did arise and that was where we stopped. But for a picnic, it seemed, we had to drive out of sight and sound of all traffic. We bounced over the uneven ground of a field. We were surrounded by rare sprigs of wild lavender and a lot of rusty tin cans. It looked like a dump, Miss Toklas commented disapprovingly. Gertrude Stein believed the dump would end soon. It didn't. So then Gertrude Stein ordained that it was not a dump and we stopped and got out. Pepe nosed around. The Kiddie cut the melon open. No one ever grew a better one or ate a better one. We consumed about a pound apiece.

Then we proceeded to Avignon. Distances in France are not great. We probably traveled less than two hundred miles. But we went back some two thousand years. After dinner Miss Toklas retired to her room. Gertrude Stein and the Kiddies walked along the Rhône. We circled the huge Palace of the Popes, fortress home of the heads of the Catholic Church in the fourteenth century. Nowadays Avignon is packed with visitors for the annual music festival. Then we had the place to ourselves.

The next day we covered a lot of ground. Les Baux, which gave the world bauxite, is a ruined medieval city set dizzily atop some cliffs. Miss Toklas stayed stubbornly in the car and enjoyed the spectacular scenery without setting eye on it. Gertrude Stein investigated a curio shop and bought two small clay animals, a cow and a donkey. They were to be put under the Kiddies' Christmas tree. We had kept ours up for the two women's Springfield visit in January. At Aigues-Mortes the three women sat in the hot dry square and sipped a sweet bottled drink. The Kiddie wandered along the top of the great old walls. In Arles, at lunch, Gertrude Stein chose white fish—"horrible fish," said Miss Toklas. We had dinner at the Pont du Gard, where a full moon shone on rock faces almost two millennia old. That was the second place well off the beaten path on this trip where a stranger asked Gertrude Stein for her autograph.

The Kiddie's old camera took postcard-size pictures. Gertrude Stein loved to be photographed and several rolls of films clicked off. And everywhere we bought melons. It was August. It was the perfect moment to pick them. We didn't have a truck. Yet when delicious melons were there for the buying, Gertrude Stein believed in buying them.

Alice B. Toklas, Gertrude Stein, and W. G. Rogers at
the Hotel Luxembourg in Nîmes.

Miss Toklas did not. Perhaps to make up for it, Miss Toklas guided the Kiddie into an antique shop. She made believe she wanted to consult him about some antique glass. She bought it.

At the town of Uzès we could have got into trouble twice with the authorities. In that sleepy place happily no authorities appeared. No one objected when Gertrude Stein steered us off the pavement onto the sidewalk. A wide arcaded walk ran around part of the public square. It was meant for window-shoppers, though to be sure there were but few windows and for that matter no shoppers. So we drove along it. It was wide, there was room, but it was not intended for autos. We may have been the first and last to ride there. A minute later no one caught us disobeying a "No Autos Allowed" sign. It was posted at the grove of trees surrounding the pavilion where Racine once wrote. Miss Toklas caught sight of the notice and called on the driver to stop. The driver obeyed. But as soon as she found out what the matter was, she went on again. "It's like a road," she said. "It is a road." It served us as a road.

Always there was this overt conflict. Gertrude Stein wanted to go left, Miss Toklas claimed right was better. They argued about the hour for departure, about feeding the dog, what to eat, where to drive, where to park, when to stop and start. There was one last disagreement, too, on the last lap of the trip. We had stopped for dinner at Vienne. We were treated to a royal feast in one of France's celebrated gourmet spots, the Restaurant of the Pyramid. It takes its name from a monument left by the Romans.

The menu consisted of pâté, freshwater crabs, chicken with truffles, salad, a *bombe* of ice cream, cakes, nuts and coffee. From there on it was one long run straight back to Bilignin. But the headlights kept shining on signs pointing to Crémieu: "Crémieu 22 kilomètres," "Crémieu 19 kilomètres" and so on. Gertrude Stein wanted to go to Crémieu. Miss Toklas exclaimed, "We do not want to go to Crémieu! Kiddie, don't let her!" We didn't get there, we went straight home. Gertrude Stein had lost another round. I don't think she cared much. Once in a great while it seemed to me she showed real annoyance. I wondered, too, whether Miss Toklas by asserting herself intended to prove she was not a mere secretary. Yet underneath all the pulling and hauling between the two women there remained a deep and abiding love.

When the Kiddies finally returned to Paris, they took enough melons to stock a store. We shared some with the landlady of our hotel and ate the rest. In *Portraits and Prayers* Gertrude Stein wrote:

> To introduce a melon, two melons, to introduce two melons, sugared melons candied melons to them, to introduce them to produce for them to send them a melon to send them to send melons two melons to them, this makes them give to you their blessing.

This adds up to far fewer melons than we collected. But it does make everybody give everybody their blessing.

20 *I know that I am the most important writer writing today.*

—EVERYBODY'S AUTOBIOGRAPHY

In the early 1930's Gertrude Stein was being published by Plain Edition. It was a shoestring operation, her shoestring and Miss Toklas'. All of a sudden she soared from the bottom of the heap to the top. By the end of the decade she was finding it hard to write enough to satisfy the demand. If publishers didn't plead "More, more!" at least they said "Yes, yes!" to her submissions. The pinch was forgotten. She had advanced from being known by a handful to being familiar to multitudes.

She found time to work despite all the diversions. There were friends to entertain in Bilignin and Paris. Just being famous kept her busy in unforeseen ways. But now there was a special urgency. It was not only that she must strike while the iron was hot. It was also that she was in her sixties. She couldn't be sure how much longer she would have. The Stein bibliography totals more than thirty volumes, including occasional duplications. From 1910 to 1935, the last year of her American tour, a period of twenty-five years, she turned out twelve titles. Thirteen more appeared posthumously. But in the eleven years years from 1936 to her death in 1946, there were eleven volumes. The climax came at the end of the war. She wrote the Kiddie:

> I've never seen anything like it, I said to Alice, we can't sell any more books because we have no more to sell, sold 4 to Italy the other day, editions in Sweden, Geneva, and now [a New York firm] wants to do my other child book To Do, the one First Reader is sold to England, to think how hard it used to be to get anybody to do anything, anyway it's nice to be glorious and popular in your old age. . . .

Following her successes with the opera, the tour and *The Autobiography of Alice B. Toklas,* she did *Everybody's Autobiography.* It consists of rich doses of general reminiscences and reflections about her youth, experiences, lecturing, writing, and friends and acquaintances. There are particularly shrewd comments on her own career. She knew what she was doing every minute she was doing it. She divided her creative years into two periods. For the later one she said, "What I did had a value that made people ready to pay." Then she continued about the earlier one: "Up to that time everything I did had a value because nobody was ready to pay." Like everything she wrote, the book was frank. But successes had softened her

191

attitudes. They were more bland and amiable. Critics were now harder to spot in the midst of her expanding army of admirers.

The two portraits she had "painted" of Picasso were complemented by a book about him in French. She did another book on a topic close at hand and equally within her special competence: *Paris France*. In the Kiddies' French copy she wrote: "To the dearest Kiddies all about our dear France and wanting the dearest Kiddies in our dear France with us Alwys Gtde & Alice." That was in 1941. We would have loved to be with them but France was no place for a rendezvous. The war was on.

It was and it wasn't all about our dear France. There are discerning insights into the French people and the author's friends among them. It is not, however, a guide-book to Paris. It is as much a guide to the heart and mind of the author. The *Picasso* is not essentially an art book, either. It tells about Picasso's struggles to get himself onto his canvases and about the birth of Cubism. You read about the year or two when he wasn't in the mood to do any painting at all. Both books would perhaps be better described under different titles. She might correctly have written not *Picasso* alone but *Picasso and Gertrude Stein* and also *Paris France and Gertrude Stein*.

Indications of her own creative processes appeared in her discussion of those of her friend. She noted, for instance, that an infant sees a face one feature at a time. It sees, say, a nose or an ear it can reach up to pull. Picasso saw a face as parts, too. He arranged them to suit his uniquely individual fancy. Gertrude Stein also saw bits

Gertrude Stein and Picasso at Bilignin in the 1930s.

and parts. Whether or not they added up to wholes, they were themselves wholes. What Picasso paints, she says in the repetitive manner of which she was a master, "is not the world the world recognizes as the world." In precisely the same terms, what she wrote is not the world the world recognizes as the world. She would, however, meet her critics halfway. She accepted their interpretation of her works . . . sometimes. At least she docilely compromised thus: "If they said I said what they said I said very likely I did."

Picasso remembered that in the early years a robber had broken into his home and stolen some clothes. He wondered ruefully whether some robber someday would realize that the paintings, too, were worth stealing. Before he became famous, he said, only a few people really understood what he was doing. After he became famous, he added wryly, still only a few people really understood. Like numerous of his contemporaries, he did not expect his paintings physically to last forever. Renaissance artists labored mightily to apply paint so it would never crack or fade or alter. Picasso did not have that goal. He wanted not the Picasso painting but the Picasso legend to last forever. It was the legend that Gertrude Stein dreamed of, too.

Her book about Paris paid a tribute to a people she had known almost all her maturity. She was there as a child; San Francisco had showed her French theater, paintings and writing. What she liked particularly about the French was their respect for her calling. "If you are a writer you have privileges," she discovered. She even got better service for her car in a garage, she claimed. The French flocked to the rue de Fleurus, and Bilignin was almost wholly French. She knew not only the residents of the Château de Béon but also the man in the street. She stopped to talk to him, too. If she was leading Basket and she didn't stop, he did. A dog is an invitation for any Frenchman to enter into a conversation. She talked to the auto mechanic, the farmer, the laborer, the clerk, the nun, the priest, the schoolteacher, the doctor and his wife. She was friends, too, with the servants. She was relaxed with them, with Hélène who worked for years at the rue de Fleurus and with successors like Trac. She gave them pats on the back. Miss Toklas gave them orders. Gertrude Stein let the reins fall slack, Miss Toklas snapped the whip.

Before we endure the trials of World War II with the two expatriates, we should consider a few works produced in those troubled years. *Ida* was brought out by a friendly but quizzical Random House. Bennett Cerf described himself on the jacket as "a publisher who rarely has the faintest idea of what Miss Stein is talking about, but who admires her from the bottom of his heart for her courage and for her abounding love of humanity and freedom." Ida is Gertrude Stein, Ida is Everywoman. Apparently unconnected incidents proliferate. A window is broken, there is an Arab, a dog is hanged, Ida wins a beauty contest, a store owner is shot, Ida is married a third time, then a fourth. And we read, too, "Let it be a lesson to her said Edith to William, but naturally William had said it first."

Mrs. Reynolds was published after the author's death. She defined what she was doing: "This book is an effort to show the way anybody could feel these years." These were the war years. Of the Reynolds husband and wife she says, "It is a perfectly ordinary couple but over them, all over them is the shadow of two men." The men are Angel Harper, representing Hitler, and Joseph Lane, who stands for Stalin.

A dramatic work that appeared later is also a product of those dreadful war years. It was Gertrude Stein's second and last opera to be produced, *The Mother of Us All*. Again Virgil Thomson, on commission from Columbia University, set it to music. It was programmed as a "pageant." It is wittier and more sophisticated than *Four Saints* and has a timelier theme. Yet it has not proved so popular, perhaps because it lacked Florine Stettheimer's designs and Frederick Ashton's choreography.

The character alluded to in the title is Susan B. Anthony, pioneer advocate of votes for women. Gertrude Stein was rarely committed to causes. She was, however, aware of this one and actively sympathetic. The characters in her far-ranging cast include Ulysses S. Grant, Thaddeus Stevens, Daniel Webster, John Adams, Lillian Russell. There are also Gertrude S. and Virgil T. While the project was under discussion, several friends who met with her were worked into the libretto. They include Donald Gallup, now her literary executor, and newsman and author Joseph Barry in the role of Jo the Loiterer.

21 *"No there will not be a war."*

The book that most feelingly describes the last tense, harrowing years is *Wars I Have Seen*. It was published in 1945. It tells of Gertrude Stein's difficulties, misfortunes, trials and occasional successes in a country again at war. The war was motivated in part by Hitler's peculiarly vicious, poisonous phobia about Jews. Gertrude Stein and Miss Toklas were Jews. They did not practice their faith. I don't remember ever hearing them discuss religion, God or a future life . . . not until Miss Toklas became a Catholic after her companion's death. But Jews they were. It could be said there was a Jewish cast to their features. Their names betrayed them, too. They could not hide their background. The French helped them in numerous ways. Otherwise they might have been caught in that monstrous satanic web that sent millions of their blood to gas chambers.

French Jews died horribly; these Americans could have, too.

"Financially there is no sense in anti-semitism. That is what I say." So Gertrude Stein wrote and believed. "How can a nation that feels itself as strong as the Germans do be afraid of a small handful of people like the Jews." Instead of any sensible answer, there was only madness.

Gertrude Stein had been absolutely sure there would not be another war. It is true that she sent the manuscripts hoarded over the decades and still in search of a publisher back to the States. They were entrusted to Carl Van Vechten. The paintings she did not bother to send. They were worth millions, or would be, but she hadn't painted them. The writing she wrote and it was hers. But she mailed it back not for fear of war but for fear she'd have to move. And she did. A year or so before Hitler invaded Poland, Gertrude Stein and Miss Toklas bade farewell to the rue de Fleurus. It had been their home for thirty-five years. It was cramped and had other disadvantages. They found a roomier place at 5 rue Christine. For a time Picasso lived just a few doors away.

Rumors of war were heard everywhere. Uneasy Parisians rioted. The appalling civil war in Spain threatened to spill over the Pyrenees into France. There were trial mobilizations on short notice. The Chasseurs Alpins, specially trained crack troops, camped in Belley. Twenty-five hundred reservists rushed into the neighborhood. Gertrude Stein lodged a score of them in her barn. In Belley, a Stein shopping center, the Croix de Feu held a nighttime rally. This rightist organization was more afraid of Communism than of Fascism, more afraid of Stalin than of Hitler . . . however mistaken that appears today. Many Croix de Feu members were Gertrude Stein's friends. She may have sympathized with them openly. She could make fun of them privately, however. She wrote a letter about the plans for a mysterious meeting. A little boy clandestinely distributed a piece of paper bearing the name of a place. When the members appeared there, a man with a handkerchief waved them on to the actual site of the rendezvous. It was like a spy thriller.

During all this uneasiness Gertrude Stein and Miss Toklas often spent idle, carefree afternoons in the fields and woods picking mushrooms. A lot of people thought there was nothing more important to be doing. They believed the blindly optimistic promise of Britain's prime minister Neville Chamberlain. His talk in Munich with Hitler meant peace in his time, he said. A friend of Gertrude Stein wrote her, "All I want is to live in the country with my wife and children." All Gertrude Stein wanted was to be left alone to write. The Kiddie nagged at her anxiously. She insisted: no war. Why? Because no one in Europe wanted one, she was sure. She told the Kiddie about a farmer in Bilignin:

> He is a gentle soul but a good soldier 42 years old, and he was mobilized, I met him just before he went with his oxen and his wife and I said M. Lambert is there going to be a war, no he said my wife is worried but no there will not be a war, why not, I said, because said he parce que c'est pas logique [because it isn't logical], what does that mean I said, well he said, I am

199

42 years old and I fought the whole war 1914–1918, my son is 18 and he would fight this war and so would I, no he said it is not logical, if I were 60 and had a grandson of 18, we would believe in war and a war might come, but I at 42 with a son of 18 no it is not logical, but said I that is alright for you but how about the germans and Italians, the same thing he said, they talk differently but they feel the same.

The farmer came back from this call-up. So they were right after all: no war. But after the next mobilization he did not come back. There was a war. Gertrude Stein in a letter to the Kiddie gracefully ate her words: "Well here we are, I never did think there would be another war for me to see and here we are, well if there is one I would of course rather be in it than out of it, there is that something about a war."

A certain nervousness is betrayed by this sentence, I think . . . and in *Wars I Have Seen* she asked, "Is it worse to be scared than to be bored." Perhaps she was just trying to reassure me and for her own part was more worried than she professed to be. That something about a war would mean hardship, deprivation and danger for her and her companion. For a time, granted, there was no shot and shell. Hitler turned his army eastward. England and France, baffled during a forlorn fall and winter, sat out what was called the phony war. Then in the spring of 1940 the Führer swung his tanks and screeching dive-bombers westward. Only an obscure young French colonel, Charles de Gaulle, knew how to stop this fearful assault. No one was listening to him then. When the Germans had attacked in 1914 they

200

were stopped at the Marne River. Nothing stopped them now. Battered remnants of the wretched British forces fled back across the Channel from Dunkerque. The French quickly surrendered.

Gertrude Stein and Miss Toklas abandoned the rue Christine. Taking only a few of the paintings, including the Picasso *Portrait*, they fled to Bilignin.

Marshal Henri Philippe Pétain of the French armies had dickered with the Germans about his country's surrender. The enemy was to occupy only the northern part of France. Frenchmen could carry on as they pleased in the rest of their land. That included Bilignin. There was some reason to approve of Pétain if by his efforts you were spared the agonizing daily presence of Nazi soldiers. But his record was reactionary. He was anti-democratic. He had saved Verdun in World War I but at a horrible cost in French lives. He had been in favor of the Maginot Line of defense erected after that war to prevent another German invasion, and it had collapsed disastrously. At the war's end the government tried him for treason and gave him a death sentence, which was later commuted to life imprisonment. His past record was forgotten in the first months after France's humiliating defeat. Furthermore, our two Americans would have noticed that Washington, playing the diplomatic game, dealt circumspectly with Pétain. Gertrude Stein worked on a friendly biographical sketch of the controversial leader but it was never finished.

While she and Miss Toklas were in the States, one treat that they particularly relished was home-canned sweet corn from my mother's farm. In the following spring I sent them carefully selected seed. They planted some every year. I hoped they would not let my good democratic corn get into the craw of any Fascists. Gertrude Stein assured me . . . perhaps a bit sharply . . . that it would not be served either to Spanish Fascists or French or Italian or German Fascists. After France's defeat there was still one season when corn could be mailed to them. But now in their beleaguered land they needed other things. Soap is customarily a wartime casualty. In every letter we included a substantial sprinkling of soapflakes. The women could no longer buy stockings yet theirs wore out. Miss Toklas couldn't buy darning cotton, either. So darning cotton padded out other envelopes.

Mrs. Kiddie had the really hard job. The two women wore underclothes as old-fashioned as their outer garments. They inhabited a cool climate and in the best of times there was hardly enough heat. Now there was less. They wanted heavy one-piece union suits with what used to be called a "barn door" in back. Mrs. Kiddie scoured New York stores from the best on Fifth Avenue to the worst in other areas. She found what they wanted. But they must have been about the last such articles left in the world of the 1940's.

When Japan's attack on Pearl Harbor plunged the United States into war, communication with our friends ceased. They were completely and hazardously on their own. They had a car but after a while they could not get gasoline. The motor was converted to run on alcohol. Then before long it stopped working and they had to give up the car. They took the train. They rode in second-class compartments where most of the windowpanes had been smashed. They could take Basket with them. He didn't have to ride in the baggage car and didn't have to be on a leash. French railways welcomed dogs as warmly as people. The two women with their dog often made the trip to Chambéry. Once in a while Gertrude Stein picked up some worn English books to read to while away the time.

They were way off in the country. Game was plentiful. But the authorities had confiscated shotguns. Lakes and ponds might be covered with tasty fat ducks but they were safe for the duration of hostilities. Gertrude Stein and Miss Toklas bought a goat. They named it Bizerte in honor of an Allied victory in North Africa. Gertrude Stein used to lead it out on a rope and let it forage for its meals. Bizerte provided milk at little cost. Everyone had to have ration tickets for food. One day in the fields a neighbor exhorted her goat, "Feed little goat feed well little goat feed without tickets." There was a black market. It was widely patronized. No one held it against the storekeeper when he was jailed for dealing in contraband. Townspeople wanted him freed quickly so they could do business with him again. When the pharmacies ran out of medicine, the peasants resorted to the herbs anciently used for many of mankind's ills. Oddly, the more baby girls were born, the more were named Madeleine. It was the custom to pin up the infants with a gold pin bearing their names. Only the name Madeleine was left on pins for sale locally. So it was Madeleine Dupont, Madeleine Legrand, Madeleine Michel and so on.

A favorite pastime of Gertrude Stein's was the consultation of prophecies. Musty old tomes revealed the prophecies of Saint Odile. Then came those of Saint Godefroy, dated 1853. The monk named Johannes had written in 1680. If you were desperately in need of encouragement, these men obligingly supplied it. Read them the way you longed to read them and France before long would drive out the enemy and Paris would be freed. You don't believe in such things? Yet Paris was liberated. These men all foretold what would happen, didn't they?

22 *One's native land is one's native land.*

—WARS I HAVE SEEN

When Gertrude Stein and Miss Toklas discovered they were definitely behind enemy lines, they also discovered they were short of money. A French friend provided all the cash needed for several months. He would not take a post-dated check or an I.O.U. Able before long to sell a painting, Gertrude Stein settled her debt with this benefactor. From then on she could meet the necessary expenses for the duration of the emergency. There had, of course, been the possibility of returning to the United States. Some people advised her to. Others urged her to retire to a safe haven in Switzerland. Both moves would have cost more than she could afford. Both also would have taken her out of the France where she really wanted to be and away from the friends on whom she depended.

Eventually the Americans had to give up their Bilignin

home. That was a blow. They were known to everyone in that village, everyone was friendly, they hated to leave. Indeed they went to law hoping to be allowed to keep their house. They lost the suit. But they had the good fortune to find a place called Le Colombier on the outskirts of Culoz. This was near their friends the d'Aiguys of the Château de Béon. The d'Aiguys were having their troubles, too. They experimented with a salad of rhubarb leaves and, said Gertrude Stein, soon wished they hadn't.

The expatriates managed to bring from Bilignin their electric hot-water heater, stove and refrigerator. They also could employ two servants . . . whom, however, they somewhat mistrusted. But they were lucky to find friends in official positions. The law required the registration of residents and particularly of Jews. When Gertrude Stein and Miss Toklas appeared at Town Hall to comply with regulations, they were told to forget it. If their names were not on official lists, the Nazis would not be so likely to spot them. This deliberate relaxation of the rules may have saved them from the worst fate imaginable. The American entry into the war made them particularly vulnerable of course. The German occupation spread over all of France. The enemy's behavior was reported to be "correct" but his presence was sorely felt.

Some neighbors' sons were drafted for labor camps inside Germany. Gertrude Stein bade them a fond farewell. Still others took to the hills and joined the resistance forces, the Maquis. At the beginning of the Occupation the French were cowed. But their spirits soon revived and their courage returned. Month by month, even in the remote department of Ain, savage underground fighters, the Maquis, made life more and more hazardous for the invader. There were bitter divisions within families and among neighbors. Anyone who catered to the foe . . . or in those turbulent times even seemed to cater . . . might get an ominous warning. He received a tiny wooden coffin. Inside it was a rope with a hangman's noose. It was a hint of future reprisal. There were in fact some summary executions when Ain finally was liberated.

These personal conflicts gave Gertrude Stein the idea for a play, *Yes Is for a Very Young Man*. It reached the public only after her death. It is not one of her most accomplished works. Nevertheless it reflects with painful accuracy the critical months in which she was living and writing. She and other Steins had often come close to war. In her childhood she saw Yankees sailing from San Francisco for the Philippines to fight in the Spanish-American War. Older relatives in Baltimore had watched Union soldiers marching to the bloody battlefields of the Civil War. Gertrude Stein wanted to expose these tragically divided loyalties. No one is wholly right, no one wholly wrong. There is reason, or a reason, on each side. If it is dreadful to bear arms, it can be almost as dreadful to be a wartime civilian among people cherishing contrary ideologies. The French had a passion for liberty. Some of them expected Pétain to provide it. Some were sure he could not. The characters in the play are a terrorist, a German, a French family and an American woman. It was produced by Lamont Johnson in the Pasadena (California) Playhouse in 1946, later in Princeton and then in New York's Cherry Lane Theatre.

Persecution, Gertrude Stein felt, made a people stronger. Deprivation made them ingenious. She raked hay. She mourned the death of her goat, Bizerte, in childbirth. She lost some chickens to the raids of hungry buzzards. She lost some supplies to hungry Germans, too. They smashed a lock and stole some food. One woman of her acquaintance had an ingenious way of getting along on a starvation diet. She pretended she was eating well. She turned it into a game. She regaled her friends with the repasts she had been enjoying only in her imagination. The truth was, her cupboard was as bare as everyone else's.

But the end was in sight. The Maquis, growing always bolder, harassed the Germans and Italians posted at the railway station. The stretch of some twelve miles from Culoz to Belley was at one time cut by as many as twenty-three roadblocks. Teams of horses hitched to German trucks hauled them through Culoz. The enemy, too, was running out of gasoline. Occupying soldiers on guard duty stayed out of sight and under cover as much as they could. One Stein sentence reports, "Six maquis attacked eight Germans killed two and the others ran away." This sentence needs commas. It can be read, "Six maquis attacked, eight Germans killed two and the others ran away." It should read, "Six maquis attacked eight Germans, killed two and the others ran away."

This author's writing had been singularly free of happenings. She now treated her readers to some drama. There was, for instance, a scuffle in Paris. A German standing on the back platform of a crowded bus stepped hard on a Frenchman's foot. Evidently it was an accident. But the angered Frenchman doubled up his fist and hit him. At once a second Frenchman hit the German a second blow. Why did he join in the fracas? He explained: "I suddenly saw a Frenchman hit out and strike a German soldier and I said hello the war must be over let me go to it and I rushed forward and hit him."

For a long time there had been a curfew, first in Bilignin and then in Culoz. Violation of it might cost a man his life. Gertrude Stein loved to walk. She sometimes put in fifteen miles a day. As dusk approached she had to keep track of the hour. She had never owned any timepiece other than clocks and an old-fashioned man's pocket watch. So now she bought a wristwatch. Then the curfew ended. Enemy guards were withdrawn from their local posts. Paris was liberated. The convincing proof of the return of peace to Culoz was a sound heard in the dead of night: someone walked down the main street whistling.

The Americans who had landed in the south of France had driven up the Rhône Valley. Now they spread out through Ain. Gertrude Stein happily went to Belley to greet an advance detachment. Eric Sevareid interviewed her on the radio. Another correspondent acted as courier to dispatch some manuscripts and letters to the States. She exulted:

> I have lived in France the best and longest part of my life and I love France and the French but after all I am an American, and it always does come back to that I was born there, and one's native land is one's native land you cannot get away from it.

Gertrude Stein and Miss Toklas rented a car to drive them back to Paris. During the nighttime ride a band of Maquis stopped them. The men in the group were unarmed; their leader, a woman, had a gun. The two passengers must show their papers. They were all in order. And what, the resistance group asked, was that big bundle in the back seat? That was a painting by Picasso. The patrol said fine and sent them on their way.

They were lucky in Paris, too. A friend told of a disaster narrowly averted. Some roving Nazis had at the last minute invaded the rue Christine apartment. They found the paintings on the walls and stacked in the corners. They complained angrily that this was, in the words of their German chiefs, "degenerate art." But they were smart enough to realize, too, how much it might be worth. They started to wrap up some canvases to cart off. The concierge interfered. They had no right to do that, she said. They paid no attention. She summoned a neighbor, who put up a stiff argument. They were not allowed to enter a private apartment without authorization from their superiors. Did they have the necessary permit? They didn't. For the moment they were foiled. Told to go and get the warrant they needed, they left. By the time they reappeared a sizable band of gendarmes had gathered. A few months before the Germans would have kicked the women out of their way. A few months before the gendarmes would not have dared oppose them. Now the Germans lost their nerve. They missed out on loot of almost immeasurable value.

The Americans invited Gertrude Stein to serve as a morale builder. She was flown to Lorraine to address vari-

A U.S. Army film recorded a G.I.'s visit with Gertrude Stein at the rue Christine in 1945. (Wide World Photos.)

ous outfits. Countless G. I.'s made her acquaintance. Word got around that she was at home to soldiers in the rue Christine, too. Droves of enlisted men and officers called on her. They showed up singly and in groups. They came at all hours of the day and night week in week out.

Her last book developed out of their conversation. She called it *Brewsie and Willie* . . . Brewsie being the nickname of a soldier she met. Her two men talk with two

American sisters, Pauline and Jane. The ideas may have been the soldiers' but many of them were plainly Gertrude Stein's, too. They discuss the Negro question, the girl question, William Jennings Bryan and Populism, Henry George and the single tax. Gertrude Stein's political and economic views were conservative. At the same time she was a free-wheeling, original thinker. She did not approve of Franklin D. Roosevelt. Having been entertained at the White House by Mrs. Eleanor Roosevelt did not change her mind, either. In *Brewsie and Willie* she tells the boys not to worry about jobs being scarce when they are discharged. Give yourselves time to think, she advises. Perhaps too much work is being done in the world. All this work exhausts a country's resources. In fact, she thinks, it might be said to waste them. She is afraid England has been impoverishing herself by her manufacturing successes. She doesn't want her own land to follow along that path. But she warns explicitly, "Dont think that communism or socialism will save you, you just have to find a new way." She does not ask more of the young men than she had asked of herself. She had found a new way in her creative field, too.

The boys kept crowding to her apartment. She loved to talk with them. Such eager visitors seemed a fresh proof that she had achieved the glory of her youthful dreams. They seemed to prove that she had become a legend. But the meetings were tiring her. The concierge posted inside the great door to the rue Christine told the soldiers more and more often that Miss Stein was not free to welcome them.

212

She had reached her seventies. She had had a hard time in the war years. Besides the physical deprivation, there was the severe nervous strain. Her stomach had been bothering her. Her cheeks were suddenly gaunt and colorless. It was a beautiful head. But in the expression of the face there was a deathly weariness.

23 *You have to learn to do everything, even to die.*

—WARS I HAVE SEEN

Gertrude Stein and Miss Toklas decided they must have a rest. Well-wishers left them no peace or quiet at the rue Christine. A friend invited them for a visit in the country. They locked up the apartment and started out. Catching sight of Picasso on a nearby corner, they stopped to talk. It was Gertrude Stein's last meeting with him.

They had not driven far when she fell seriously ill. She could no longer ignore a persistent digestive disorder. They turned back at once. Gertrude Stein entered the American Hospital in Neuilly, a suburb that except for a line on the map is Paris itself. She had an abdominal tumor. Apparently she understood the ultimate dreadful alternatives. Without an operation she would probably die. With an operation she would probably die. She chose the operation.

To console her there was the presence of the devoted

214

One of the last photographs of Gertrude Stein, with Basket and Marie Laurencin's portrait of him.

Miss Toklas. There were also copies, newly arrived, of *Brewsie and Willie*. Miss Toklas sat with her. Gertrude Stein, her mind churning as it had all her life, asked, "What is the answer?" Miss Toklas was silent. Gertrude Stein asked, "In that case, what is the question?" Miss Toklas in her book *What Is Remembered* concludes her account of this heartbreaking moment: "They took her away on a wheeled stretcher to the operating room and I never saw her again." That was the afternoon of Saturday, July 27, 1946. Cables to Carl Van Vechten, to Donald Gallup and to me, the Kiddie, told of her death.

Burial took place in Père Lachaise Cemetery. It is the resting place of many French artists and writers. The tombstone was designed by a painter friend, Sir Francis Rose. Room also was reserved there for Miss Toklas. The stone bears the date July 29 instead of 27. It gives the birthplace as "Allfghany." So to the very end and beyond, write and right had little in common. The spelling that had always been uncertain remained uncertain.

Miss Toklas lived twenty-one years more. Some of those years were harried, too. According to Gertrude Stein's will, the paintings were bequeathed to Allan, son of Michael and Sarah Stein. But they would go to him only after two other purposes had been served. First, the unpublished writing must be published. What had not been commercially profitable in Gertrude Stein's lifetime was still unacceptable to trade publishers. She left several thousand dollars in cash. If that was not enough, a painting or paintings should be sold. In the second place, Miss Toklas was to be amply provided for. If that, too, meant the sale of more paintings, then again they were to be sold.

The remaining writing was published in eight volumes by the Yale University Press; for the author this was the seal of distinction. Carl Van Vechten was the editor. Each book had a foreword by a friend or acquaintance: Janet Flanner of *The New Yorker* magazine, Natalie Clifford Barney, Daniel-Henry Kahnweiler, the art dealer, and others.

216

There still remained the serious problem of Miss Toklas' livelihood. She was most reluctant to break up the art collection left by her dear companion. Yet for a time she found it very hard, indeed impossible, to pay the landlord or the grocer. Some friends came discreetly to her rescue and helped with doctor's bills. At last she sold a series of a score or more of Picasso prints. She called Picasso to ask what their market value was. He suggested several thousand dollars. Accordingly that was the sum she received. Then a dealer began selling each individual print for the amount given for the entire lot. Had Picasso underestimated their value? Had Miss Toklas misunderstood him? Besides this unfortunate incident, the paintings were being left without adequate protection in the rue Christine apartment. The concierge was not a competent watchman. Even if Miss Toklas were there, thieves could have carted away a fortune. But Miss Toklas often was not there. She was not well. The Paris apartment was not warm enough in her old age. She went to Italy for a cure at a watering place. She spent a winter or two in a convent in Rome. The paintings could not be insured because the cost would have been prohibitive.

As a result Gertrude Stein's heirs appealed to the courts for the protection of their rights. Their action was understandable. It is also understandable that a good deal of ill feeling was generated. The paintings must be placed for safekeeping in a bank vault, the courts ruled. Miss Toklas moved from the rue Christine to a modern apartment on the rue de la Convention. It was technically Left Bank but it was a Right Bank bourgeois neighborhood. It was well

Alice B. Toklas in 1952, a portrait by Dora Maar.

down the river from the part of the city Miss Toklas knew so well. You climbed a splendid curving staircase to the rue Christine home. The new place boasted of an elevator, not so grand but much more useful. There were clean, hygienically white walls. They were completely bare of paintings. She had loved the paintings, the painters, the collector most of all. The paintings had been her constant companions for most of her adult life. Not one was left.

With her finances now in order, she had the services of a maid and a cook. One trouble was, she said wryly, the cook could not cook. She turned Catholic and that was a great comfort to her. She wrote *The Alice B. Toklas Cook Book*. It was followed by *Aromas and Flavors of Past and Present*, with an introduction and comments by Poppy Cannon, an author well known in the cookbook field. The recipes had a certain exotic character. If they were not tried in the kitchen, they were discussed there, and in the parlor and study as well. Following these books there came Miss Toklas' memoirs, smartly titled *What Is Remembered*. What was remembered was, after a summary of the early Californian years, the life the two women had led together and their innumerable encounters among artists and writers. Miss Toklas was more impressed than her companion by money and social position. But most of all she was indelibly impressed by her companion. The book is . . . purposely or not purposely . . . a tribute to Gertrude Stein. You have only to consider the illustrations to appreciate this. Among them are thirteen pictures of the two women together, fourteen pictures of Gertrude Stein alone, and two pictures of Miss Toklas alone.

The Stein estate had two literary executors, Van Vechten and Dr. Donald Gallup, curator of the Collection of American Literature at Yale's Beinecke Library. Miss Toklas stepped into the position of eventual arbiter. The woman who began as a typist friend ended as the final judge of matters pertaining to Gertrude Stein. It was a promotion she deserved. But her health failed. She lost her eyesight and her hearing. The last time I saw her was a year before her death. She was practically bedridden. She died on March 7, 1967. She was buried beside Gertrude Stein.

The fine plain headstone is the width of the two graves. Miss Toklas' name and the dates . . . the correct dates . . . are on the back. When I last visited it, two withered bouquets lay on top of the stone and one artificial rose had been stuck in the dirt at the foot of it. The lettering on the front was all but illegible; the marks of the stonecutter's chisel were almost obliterated. So in the end the spelling really doesn't matter at all.

The Stein story went grandly on. There were full-length biographies plus exhaustive studies. A one-woman reading, *Gertrude Stein's Gertrude Stein,* was staged by the American actress Nancy Cole in Paris, London, Edinburgh and many American universities. *The Mother of Us All* enjoyed a revival thanks in part to its relevance to the cause of woman's liberation. Some Gertrude Stein nonsense prose was developed into an Off-Broadway show. Her life was the subject of a television program. The Museum of Modern Art in New York presented an unusually popular all-Stein exhibition. It included works once owned by Gertrude, Leo, Michael and Sarah Stein. It traveled to other cities.

Gertrude Stein's own collection at her death consisted of thirty-eight paintings by Picasso and nine by Juan Gris. Four men, all connected with the Museum of Modern Art, chipped in more than six million dollars to buy it. The purchasers were John Hay Whitney, William S. Paley, New York governor Nelson Rockefeller, and André Mayer. It is understood that each will eventually leave to the Museum one of the works that fell to his lot.

According to a very rough estimate, they paid more than $125,000 apiece for the pictures. Gertrude Stein's average payment was certainly less than $1,000 apiece. For a woman supposedly too impractical to earn her own living, that was doing pretty well.

Miss Toklas, as a Catholic, was confident she would join Gertrude Stein in a better world. Gertrude Stein held the belief of many of her French friends. In *Paris France* she wrote of "the way they feel about the dead, it is so friendly so simply friendly and though inevitable not a sadness and though occurring not a shock." She believed firmly that "dead is dead." She was right, she was wrong. The woman is dead, the writing lives.

Selected Bibliography

Many articles, pamphlets, booklets and catalogs have been devoted to Gertrude Stein. There are, for instance, Jane Mayhall's understanding essay on *Things As They Are* in *Rediscoveries*, edited by David Madden and published by Crown in 1971; the Museum of Modern Art catalog, "Four Americans in Paris: The Collections of Gertrude Stein and her Family," with a foreword by John B. Hightower and an introduction by Margaret Potter, published by the museum in 1970; "Testimony Against Gertrude Stein," by Georges Braque and others, a *transition* magazine supplement published in Paris in 1935.

She figures in many books, as, for instance, Edmund Wilson's *Upstate: Records and Recollections of Northern New York*, published by Farrar, Straus and Giroux in 1971; in John Glasco's *Memoirs of Montparnasse*, published by Oxford University Press in 1970; in Ernest Hemingway's *A Moveable Feast*, published by Charles Scribner's Sons in 1964. Stein autographs were collected in a pamphlet; numerous theater programs contain helpful information.

The bulk of the material about her, however, is found in two kinds of books: those she wrote and those written about her.

BOOKS BY GERTRUDE STEIN (in the order in which they were published):

Three Lives. New York: The Modern Library, 1933 (originally published in 1909)

Tender Buttons. New York: Claire-Marie, 1914

Geography and Plays (introduced by Sherwood Anderson). Boston: The Four Seas Co., 1922

The Making of Americans. Paris: Contact Editions, 1925 (New York: Harcourt, Brace & Co., abridged edition, 1934)

Composition as Explanation. London: The Hogarth Press, 1928

Useful Knowledge. New York: Payson and Clarke, 1928

Lucy Church Amiably. Paris: Plain Edition, 1930

Before the Flowers of Friendship Faded Friendship Faded. Paris: Plain Edition, 1931

How to Write. Paris: Plain Edition, 1932

Operas and Plays. Paris: Plain Edition, 1932

The Autobiography of Alice B. Toklas. New York: Harcourt, Brace & Co., 1933

Portraits and Prayers. New York: Random House, 1934

Lectures in America. New York: Random House, 1935

Narration (introduction by Thornton Wilder). Chicago: University of Chicago Press, 1935

The Geographical History of America (introduction by Thornton Wilder). New York: Random House, 1936

Everybody's Autobiography. New York: Random House, 1937

Picasso. London: Batsford, 1938

The World Is Round. New York: William R. Scott, 1939

Paris France. New York: Charles Scribner's Sons, 1940
What Are Masterpieces (foreword by Robert Bartlett Haas).
Los Angeles: The Conference Press, 1940
Ida, A Novel. New York: Random House, 1944
Wars I Have Seen. New York: Random House, 1945
Brewsie and Willie. New York: Random House, 1946
Selected Writings of Gertrude Stein (edited and with introduction and notes by Carl Van Vechten). New York: Random House, 1946
The Gertrude Stein First Reader and Three Plays. Dublin and London: Maurice Fridberg, 1946
Four in America (introduction by Thornton Wilder). New Haven: Yale University Press, 1947
Last Operas and Plays (introduction by Carl Van Vechten). New York: Rinehart and Co., 1949
Things As They Are. Pawlet, Vermont: The Banyan Press, 1951
Two: Gertrude Stein and Her Brother (foreword by Janet Flanner). New Haven: Yale University Press, 1951
Mrs. Reynolds (foreword by Lloyd Frankenberg). New Haven: Yale University Press, 1952
Bee Time Vine (introduction by Virgil Thomson). New Haven: Yale University Press, 1953
As Fine As Melanctha (foreword by Natalie Clifford Barney). New Haven: Yale University Press, 1954
Painted Lace (introduction by Daniel-Henry Kahnweiler). New Haven: Yale University Press, 1955
Stanzas in Meditation (preface by Donald Sutherland). New Haven: Yale University Press, 1956
Alphabets and Birthdays (introduction by Donald Gallup). New Haven: Yale University Press, 1957
A Novel of Thank You (introduction by Carl Van Vechten). New Haven: Yale University Press, 1958

BOOKS ABOUT GERTRUDE STEIN

Bridgman, Richard, *Gertrude Stein in Pieces.* New York: Oxford University Press, 1970

Brinnin, John Malcolm, *The Third Rose: Gertrude Stein and Her World.* Boston: Atlantic–Little, Brown, 1959

Gallup, Donald, editor, *The Flowers of Friendship: Letters Written to Gertrude Stein.* New York: Alfred A. Knopf, 1953

Miller, Rosalind S., *Gertrude Stein: Form and Intelligibility* (containing the Radcliffe themes). New York: Exposition Press, 1949

Olivier, Fernande, *Picasso et ses amis.* Paris: Stock, 1933

Pollack, Barbara, *The Collectors: Dr. Claribel and Miss Etta Cone.* Indianapolis and New York: Bobbs-Merrill, 1962

Reid, B. L., *Art by Subtraction: A Dissenting Opinion of Gertrude Stein.* Norman: University of Oklahoma Press, 1958

Rogers, W. G., *When This You See Remember Me: Gertrude Stein in Person.* New York: Rinehart and Co., 1948 (Indianapolis and New York: Bobbs-Merrill Charter Books, 1964; Westport, Connecticut: Greenwood Press, 1971)

Sprigge, Elizabeth, *Gertrude Stein: Her Life and Work.* New York: Harper & Brothers, 1957

Stein, Leo, *The A-B-C of Aesthetics.* New York: Boni & Liveright, 1927

——, *Appreciation: Painting, Poetry and Prose.* New York: Crown Publishers, 1950

——, *Journey into the Self: Being the Letters, Papers and Journals of Leo Stein* (edited by Edmund Fuller, introduction by Van Wyck Brooks). New York: Crown Publishers, 1950

Sutherland, Donald, *Gertrude Stein: A Biography of Her Work.* New Haven: Yale University Press, 1951

Toklas, Alice B., *The Alice B. Toklas Cook Book.* New York: Harper & Brothers, 1954

———, *Aromas and Flavors of Past and Present* (with introduction and comment by Poppy Cannon). New York: Harper & Brothers, 1958

———, *What Is Remembered.* New York: Holt, Rinehart & Winston, 1963

Index

229

230

233

236

About the Author

W. G. Rogers was one of the first of the many American soldiers whom Gertrude Stein was to befriend in the course of two wars, but in his case a chance meeting in the south of France in 1917 led to a long and dear friendship.

Mr. Rogers was born in Springfield, Massachusetts, and was graduated as a Phi Beta Kappa from Amherst College. For nearly twenty years he was books and arts editor of the Associated Press, and he is now associate editor of the Saturday Review Syndicate. Mr. Rogers is the author of *When This You See Remember Me: Gertrude Stein in Person; Carl Sandburg, Yes; Wise Men Fish Here: The Story of Frances Steloff and the Gotham Book Mart;* and many other books, including surveys of modern painting and architecture for young readers, and (with his wife, the poet Mildred Weston) *Carnival Crossroads: The Story of Times Square.*

The Rogerses now live in the mountainous country of western Pennsylvania, and Mr. Rogers says his only hobby is getting to Paris and staying as long as he can.

This book may be kept

FOURTEEN DAYS

A fine will be charged for each day the book is kept overtime.

GAYLORD 142			PRINTED IN U.S.A.